Step Up to Writing

Three Levels of Learning!

Grades 3–5

by Elizabeth Suarez Aguerre and Jenifer Soler Batchelder

Carson-Dellosa Publishing Company, Inc. • Greensboro, North Carolina

Credits

Content Editor: Ginny Swinson

Copy Editor: Jennifer Weaver-Spencer

Layout Design, Cover Design, and Inside Illustrations: Lori Jackson

This book has been correlated to state, national, and Canadian provincial standards. Visit *www.carsondellosa.com* to search for and view its correlations to your standards.

ISBN 978-0-69200-200-1

Table of Contents

About This Book

Purpose

Teaching student writers to become better authors can be a challenging task, even for experienced teachers. *Step Up to Writing* provides quick and clear mini-lessons, each followed by three student activity pages already adapted for three levels of learning: Basic, Intermediate, and Challenging. Start students off with the activity pages that match their learning levels in writing. Students will steadily gain the knowledge and confidence they need to become good writers. You will be satisfied knowing that you have taken an important step toward building the writing skills your students need for success.

What Is Differentiated Instruction?

Differentiated instruction is an educational methodology that uses modified instruction to meet the needs of each student. These modifications involve offering multiple approaches to content, instruction, and assessment. Because students have a range of ability levels, differentiation allows all students to maximize their strengths. Challenging and supporting all students through differentiated instruction can result in increased motivation and learning.

How Can Educators Effectively Differentiate Instruction?

Acknowledging that students learn in different ways is the first step toward differentiating instruction. Teachers can differentiate instruction in the following ways:

- Offer multiple methods for students to demonstrate success.
- Provide a variety of materials at multiple levels to address different learning styles.
- Tailor assignments to meet each student's needs.
- Allow each student to work at his own pace.
- Support each student by giving individual help as needed.
- Provide learning tasks at appropriate levels of difficulty.

Step Up to Writing includes learning activities that offer students opportunities to develop core skills and demonstrate individual strengths.

In This Book

You can choose to target specific a skill using one of 35 mini-lessons. Every mini-lesson is followed by three levels of activity pages to reinforce each skill. The number of circles at the bottom of each activity page indicates the level of the activity:

Level One: Basic   Level Two: Intermediate   Level Three: Challenging

How to Use This Book

Use *Step Up to Writing* to teach writing in the way that is most comfortable for you.

- Teach according to the four core elements of good writing: Organization, Ideas and Content, Word Choice and Voice, and Conventions.
    - Use the Table of Contents to identify and select lessons based on the order in which you prefer to teach.
    - Progress through the book in sequential order in each unit.

- Teach by writing mode: Narrative, Expository, Persuasive, Poetry, Letter Writing, and Descriptive. Refer to the Skills Matrix on pages 6–7 to see a complete list of page numbers and corresponding writing modes. You can also quickly identify lessons with appropriate writing modes by looking at the codes at the bottom of each mini-lesson page.

Sample: **N, E, PER, PO, L, D** | **109**

Writing Mode Code Letters

N Narrative	E Expository	PER Persuasive
PO Poetry	L Letter Writing	D Descriptive

- Teach by aligning writing skills with reading skills. For example, when teaching sequencing in a reading comprehension lesson, you can reinforce the skill with a writing lesson on time-order words and phrases.

How to Differentiate Writing Instruction Using This Book

- Assign each student a leveled activity page. For example, you can assign Level One (Basic) activity pages to struggling learners and assign Level Two (Intermediate) and Level Three (Challenging) activities to advanced learners. Then, assign Intermediate and Advanced activity pages as appropriate.
- Have all students focus on the same skill while working at one of three ability levels.
- Use the mini-lessons in whole-class or small-group instruction. Use the three levels to form flexible groups for targeted instruction.
- For further differentiation, use the extension activities included in many mini-lessons to offer additional practice or to widen the scope of a skill. Look for the star icon to identify these extensions.
- Refer to the book lists provided at the end of most mini-lessons to tie applicable, authentic children's literature to specific writing skills. The complete list of children's literature can be found on page 153. Look for the open book icon to identify these book lists.

Skills Matrix

A ★ on the Skills Matrix specifies the writing mode that is used for each worksheet or mini-lesson. A ✔ indicates an additional mode to which the mini-lesson can be applied. (Mini-lessons are indicated on the Skills Matrix with **M** beside the page number.)

Page Number	Narrative	Expository	Persuasive	Poetry	Letter Writing	Descriptive
8M	✔	★	✔			✔
9		★				★
10		★				
11		★				
12M	★					
14	★					
15	★					
16	★					
17M	★					
19	★					
20	★					
21	★					
22M	★	✔	✔			
23	★					
24	★					
25	★					
26M	★	✔	✔	✔		✔
27	★	★				
28	★					
29		★				★
30M	★	✔	✔		✔	
31	★					
32	★					
33	★					
34M	★	✔	✔		✔	

Page Number	Narrative	Expository	Persuasive	Poetry	Letter Writing	Descriptive
35	★	★				
36	★					
37	★					
38M	✔	★	✔			
39		★				
40		★				
41		★				
42M	✔	★	✔	✔		✔
44		★				
45		★				
46		★				
47M		★				
48		★				
49		★				
50		★				
51M			★			
52		★				
53		★				
54		★				
55M				★		★
56				★		★
57				★		★
58				★		★
59M					★	
61		★				

Page Number	Narrative	Expository	Persuasive	Poetry	Letter Writing	Descriptive
62					★	
63					★	
64M					★	
65					★	
66					★	
67					★	
68M	★	✔	✔	✔		✔
69	★					
70	★					
71	★	★				
72M	★	✔	✔			
73	★					
74	★					
75	★					
76M	★	✔	✔	✔		
77	★					
78	★					
79	★					
80M	★					★
81	★					★
82	★					★
83	★					★
84M	★					★
85						★
86						★

Skills Matrix, continued

Page Number	Narrative	Expository	Persuasive	Poetry	Letter Writing	Descriptive
87	★	★				★
88M	★	✓	✓	✓		✓
89						★
90	★					★
91	★					★
92M	★					✓
93	★					★
94	★					★
95	★					★
96M	✓	✓	✓		★	
97	★	★			★	
98		★	★			
99			★	★		
100M	★	✓		✓		
102	★					
103	★					
104	★					
105M	★					★
106	★					★
107	★					★
108	★					★
109M	✓	✓	✓	✓	✓	★
110						★
111						★
112						★
113M	✓	✓	✓	✓	✓	★
114						★
115						★
116						★

Page Number	Narrative	Expository	Persuasive	Poetry	Letter Writing	Descriptive
117M	✓	✓	✓	✓		★
118						★
119						★
120						★
121M	✓	✓		✓		★
122						★
123						★
124						★
125M	★	✓		✓		✓
126						★
127						★
128						★
129M	★			✓		★
130	★					★
131	★					★
132	★					★
133M	★	★	★		★	
134	★					
135	★					
136	★					
137M	★	★	★		★	★
138	★	★				
139		★				
140	★	★				
141M	✓	✓	✓	✓	✓	★
142	★					
143	★					
144	★					
145M	★					

Page Number	Narrative	Expository	Persuasive	Poetry	Letter Writing	Descriptive
146	★					
147	★					
148	★					
149M	★	✓	✓			
150	★	★				
151	★					
152	★					

A paragraph typically consists of several sentences that support a single topic. Writing a complete paragraph helps organize the author's thoughts and ideas. Using a burger graphic organizer will help students write detailed paragraphs.

Mini-Lesson:

- Tell students about a delicious burger you recently had for dinner. Describe the toasted bun, the burger, the crisp lettuce, and the red tomato.

- Ask students what might have happened if the juicy burger or the top bun had been left off. Explain that you would not have been satisfied because your burger would have been incomplete.

- Tell students that writing a paragraph is like building a burger.

- Show students the example. Identify the sentences that represent each part of the burger.

The topic sentence tells what a paragraph is about.
My miniature poodle, Cookie, has recently learned a variety of amusing tricks.

The details tell about the topic.
Whenever she wants me to take her for a walk, she pulls her leash from the hook in the hall. She waits by the door with the leash dangling from her teeth until I take her out. She also lifts her right paw and taps me on the leg when she wants my attention. Cookie even rolls over on her back and howls softly so that I will rub her belly.

The conclusion helps hold everything together.
Her tricks keep me laughing all day long!

Extension

Model writing a new paragraph. Have students come to the board and circle the sentences that represent each part of the burger.

Paragraph Structure

A **paragraph** is a group of sentences that tell about one idea. It contains a topic sentence, details and examples about the topic, and a conclusion.

Use the details to write a topic sentence for the beginning of each paragraph.

Paragraph 1

My sister helps me wash the dishes, even if it's not her turn to do chores. If I am having trouble with my homework, she helps me figure it out. My sister also lets me have the last slice of pizza at dinner, even if she'd like to have it for herself!

I am very lucky to have such a kind sister.

Paragraph 2

During the spring, flowers begin to bloom. Their sweet smell fills the air. You can hear birds chirping in the trees. The breeze makes it perfect weather for picnics and kite flying.

Spring is a delightful time of year.

Extra: Replace the conclusion in each paragraph.

1. _____

2. _____

Name _____   Date _____

Paragraph Structure

A **paragraph** is a group of sentences that tell about one idea. It contains a topic sentence, details and examples about the topic, and a conclusion.

Number the sentences in order in each paragraph.

Paragraph 1

_____ They find dens or caves to hibernate in.

_____ Hibernating is important because it helps bears survive a season when food is limited.

_____ Hibernation is a major part of a black bear's life.

_____ Black bears remain in a sleeplike condition throughout the winter months.

_____ When it is hibernating, a bear's body temperature drops about 10 degrees.

Paragraph 2

_____ They eat nuts and berries.

_____ Eating both plants and animals helps bears get the nutrition they need.

_____ Black bears are omnivores.

_____ They eat both plants and animals.

_____ Insects, from ants to termites, are also an important part of their diet.

_____ Many bears catch fish, such as salmon, from rivers and streams.

   Step Up to Writing · CD-104384 · © Carson-Dellosa

Paragraph Structure

> A **paragraph** is a group of sentences that tell about one idea. It contains a topic sentence, details and examples about the topic, and a conclusion.

Read each topic sentence and conclusion. Write three detailed sentences to support each topic and complete each paragraph.

Paragraph 1

Saturday afternoons are my favorite part of the week.

_____

_____

_____

_____

_____

I am always excited when I wake up on Saturday mornings!

Paragraph 2

An awesome party must have several things.

_____

_____

_____

_____

_____

These things would help create an unforgettable party.

 Extra: Draw a burger organizer on another sheet of paper and use it to plan a paragraph.

Mini-Lesson

Beginning, Middle, and End

A narrative should include organized writing that creates a comprehensible story line. Learning that a story should have a beginning, a middle, and an end will help students avoid creating obscure characters and incomplete plots. Understanding how a story is put together will help students create unified narratives. After students understand how to identify and write a complete story line, they will learn to improve the quality of their writing with skills such as elaboration (Unit 2) and personification (Unit 3).

Key Story Components

Beginning (Introduction)	Middle (Body)	End (Conclusion)
• Introduces characters and tells what happens first • Ask: Who are the characters? What are they doing?	• Contains most of the action and may state a problem • Ask: What is the story about? What is the problem?	• Completes the story and may solve the problem • Ask: How is the problem solved? What happens to the characters?

Mini-Lesson:

• Tell students that you will read a story to them. Tell them that they should think about what happens in the beginning, in the middle, and at the end.

• Read aloud a story with a clear beginning, middle, and end. The example used on page 13 is *Thunder Cake* by Patricia Polacco.

• Draw a three-column chart on the board similar to the chart above. Label the columns *Beginning*, *Middle*, and *End*.

• Guide students to fill in each column. For the *Beginning* column, ask questions such as: What happens at the beginning of the story? Whom do we meet? What do they want to do? For the *Middle* column, ask: What is the problem? What are the characters doing? For the *End* column, ask: How is the problem solved? How do the characters feel?

• As students provide answers, locate the sections to which they are referring. This will remind students of the key points in the plot and emphasize the organization of the story. Then, write students' comments in the appropriate columns. Refer to the completed chart on page 13.

Thunder Cake by Patricia Polacco

Beginning	Middle	End
• A little girl and her grandmother live on a farm in Michigan. • The girl is scared of thunder. • They decide to bake a Thunder Cake.	• They count how far away the storm is. • They get eggs from Nellie Peck Hen. • They get milk from old Kick Cow. • They get sugar and chocolate from the shed. • They pick tomatoes and cherries. • They bake the cake.	• The storm came. • They ate the cake. • The girl realized that she had been brave all along.

- Discuss how the story would be incomplete if the beginning, middle, or end were missing. For example, ask students what the story would be like if it began when the characters were gathering ingredients or if it ended before the thunderstorm.
- Tell students that each story they write must have a beginning, a middle, and an end.

Extension

For higher-level students, use terminology such as *introduction*, *development*, and *resolution* instead of *beginning*, *middle*, and *end*.

Book List

Examples of beginning, middle, and end can be found in *Lilly's Purple Plastic Purse*, *The Paper Bag Princess*, *Red Riding Hood* (traditional version), and *The True Story of the 3 Little Pigs*.

Beginning, Middle, and End

A story should have a beginning, a middle, and an end. These parts help the reader follow the story line without getting confused. The **beginning** of a story usually introduces the characters. The **middle** is where the plot of the story unfolds, and a problem may be presented. The **end** completes the story and may solve the problem.

Look at the chart. The beginning and the end of a story about a boy named Charlie have been written for you. Write four events that could happen in the middle of the story.

Beginning

Charlie finally climbed into his warm bed. He wanted to forget about the math test he had to take on Friday. He hoped that he would get a good night's sleep. As soon as he rested his head on his pillow, he fell asleep. Unfortunately, Charlie had an eventful night.

Middle

1. _____

_____

2. _____

_____

3. _____

_____

4. _____

_____

End

Charlie quickly sat up in bed. His forehead was damp with sweat, and he could feel his knees trembling under the covers. His bad dream was over.

 Extra: Create a new ending to the story. Write it on another sheet of paper.

Beginning, Middle, and End

A story should have a beginning, a middle, and an end. These parts help the reader follow the story line without getting confused. The **beginning** of a story usually introduces the characters. The **middle** is where the plot of the story unfolds, and a problem may be presented. The **end** completes the story and may solve the problem.

In this story, a girl named Lucy is afraid of monsters. The middle of the story has been written for you. Write a beginning and an end to complete the story.

Beginning

_____

_____

_____

_____

_____

Middle

   "Tonight," Lucy proclaimed, "I will face my fears!" As Lucy was getting ready for bed, she took the flashlight out of her dresser drawer. Lucy carefully tucked the flashlight under her pillow and climbed into bed. She waited a few minutes before she whispered, "OK, it's now or never. I must find out if creatures really are hiding under my bed." Lucy took a deep breath, grabbed the flashlight, and braced herself. She sprang out of bed and shouted, "Here I come!" Lucy flashed the bright beam of light under the bed. "Just as I suspected," she laughed.

End

_____

_____

_____

_____

_____

Beginning, Middle, and End

A story should have a beginning, a middle, and an end. These parts help the reader follow the story line without getting confused. The **beginning** of a story usually introduces the characters. The **middle** is where the plot of the story unfolds, and a problem may be presented. The **end** completes the story and may solve the problem.

A good friend is someone whom you can count on. But, even best friends can have disagreements. Imagine that you are writing a story about two friends who have a disagreement. Use the chart to list the main events in the beginning, middle, and end of your story.

Beginning
_____
_____
_____
_____
_____
Middle
_____
_____
_____
_____
_____
End
_____
_____
_____
_____
_____

Plot Development

Mini-Lesson

The plot of a story is a series of related events. It is the most exciting part of a story and includes events that enhance the conflict. Developing a plot that holds the reader's attention can be challenging. Once students have gained an understanding of basic story elements—character, setting, problem, and solution—they should learn how to make connections among them.

Mini-Lesson:

- Begin by asking students what it feels like to be the new child in school, on a sports team, in the neighborhood, or at a party. Discuss how everyone can relate to feeling shy, nervous, or excited. Have students share personal experiences.

- Tell students that they will help plan a story about a new child in school. The child is shy but wants to make new friends. Tell students that they will focus on creating the plot. Explain that a story's plot includes the problem or conflict that a character is facing and how the character tries to solve it. Emphasize that the plot is the most interesting and exciting part of the story.

- Create a flowchart on the board. (See the example on page 18.) Have students decide on the setting of the story and name the main character. Then, guide students into writing the problem and the solution on the chart. At this point, do not fill in the events that lead to the conclusion.

- Show students an example of how the story would sound if the main character solved the problem quickly. (See the example on the right.)

> Catherine wanted to make friends at her new school. She sat next to Lisa at lunch, and they became friends.

- Help students understand that to write a clear plot, they should make connections between the problem and the solution.

- Have students help you write on the chart the three events that lead to the conclusion.

Plot Development, continued

Setting: Meadow Walk Elementary School

Character: Catherine, a fourth-grade student

Problem: Catherine is very shy. She is worried about being at a new school. She wants to make friends, but she is afraid that no one will like her.

Event 1: On the bus to school, she sits beside a boy who ignores her.

Event 2: While at the library, she tries to talk to a girl in her class, but the librarian tells them that they are not allowed to talk.

Event 3: During lunch, she sits at a table with her classmates and starts a conversation with a girl named Lisa.

Solution: Catherine and Lisa become friends.

Plot Development

The **plot** is what happens in a story. A strong plot includes not only the problem and a solution but also a series of events that leads to the ending.

Brandon is being teased by an older boy. Complete a writing plan for a story that describes how Brandon solves his problem. Fill in the flowchart with the third event that leads to the conclusion. Use the flowchart to help you write the story on another sheet of paper.

Setting: Broad Oaks Park

Characters: Brandon, an 8-year-old boy   Joe, a 12-year-old boy

Problem: Brandon is being teased by Joe, an older boy.

Event 1:
That night, Brandon tells his dad what happened.

Event 2:
Brandon asks his dad for advice.

Event 3: _____
_____
_____
_____
_____
_____
_____
_____

Solution: Joe does not tease Brandon anymore. Now, they both enjoy playing in the park.

Plot Development

The **plot** is what happens in a story. A strong plot includes not only the problem and a solution but also a series of events that leads to the ending.

Many children believe that they should have later bedtimes. Complete a writing plan for a story about a girl who tries to get her parents to let her stay up an hour past her bedtime. Fill in the missing details on the flowchart. Use the flowchart to help you write the story on another sheet of paper.

Setting: _____

↓

Characters: _____

↓

Problem: _____ would like to have a later bedtime. She would like to stay up an hour later each night.

Event 1: _____
_____
_____
_____
_____

Event 2: _____
_____
_____
_____
_____
_____

Event 3: _____
_____
_____
_____
_____
_____

Solution: Her parents allow her to stay up an extra hour on Friday and Saturday nights only.

Plot Development

The **plot** is what happens in a story. A strong plot includes not only the problem and a solution but also a series of events that leads to the ending.

Sometimes, it can be difficult to get along with a younger brother or sister. Create a writing plan for a story about a child who is annoyed by a younger brother or sister and how the child deals with the situation. Fill in the details on the flowchart. Use the flowchart to help you write the story on another sheet of paper.

Setting: _____

Characters: _____

Problem: _____
_____

Event 1: _____
_____
_____
_____
_____
_____

Event 2: _____
_____
_____
_____
_____
_____

Event 3: _____
_____
_____
_____
_____
_____

Solution: _____
_____

Mini-Lesson

Terrific Beginnings, Part One

Good authors grab the reader's attention from the start. An interesting beginning encourages the reader to continue reading. Knowing a variety of opening strategies will help students write interesting beginnings.

Mini-Lesson:

- Ask students what they do when they begin reading a book with a boring beginning. Does the beginning motivate them to continue reading?

- Explain to students that good authors grab the reader's attention from the start. A terrific beginning makes the reader want to read more.

- Tell students to imagine writing a story about a time when they went on a trip.

- Write this sentence on the board:

My trip to Tigercat Stadium was great.

Ask students if they think that this is a terrific beginning.

- Present two strategies for great beginnings: using action and using dialogue. Use the examples or have students help you create new beginnings based on these strategies.

| **Action:** The quarterback tightly grips the ball. He spots a wide receiver in the distance. The quarterback launches the ball in the air. Touchdown! The Tigercats have scored. | **Dialogue:** "Chris, I found our seats!" I shouted as we approached the first row. "This view is amazing. I can see all of the players warming up for the game. I know they will win today!" My trip to Tigercat Stadium was just getting started. |

Book List

Examples of great beginnings can be found in *Because of Winn-Dixie, Charlotte's Web, Ramona the Pest,* and *A Taste of Blackberries.*

Terrific Beginnings, Part One

Good authors grab the reader's attention from the start. A **terrific beginning** will make the reader want to continue reading.

Read each pair of story beginnings. Decide which beginning is terrific. Write *yes* if the beginning is terrific. Write *no* if the beginning is not terrific.

1. A. _____   My brother and I race down the stairs with our duffel bags. He skips the last step and beats me, but I'm not far behind. We hear Dad start the engine. I step outside, and Mom locks the door behind me. This is where our adventure begins.

   B. _____   My family and I are going on a road trip. It will be a great adventure.

2. A. _____   "Mom, can we please go to the movies later today?" I asked for the third time. "Not today," she answered firmly. "On Sundays we stay home and relax." I knew that I would not change her mind. Sunday afternoons at home are so dull.

   B. _____   There is never anything to do on Sundays. Sunday is a very dull day.

3. A. _____   Baseball is a terrific game. It is very exciting. I love to play baseball because it is something that I do well.

   B. _____   I step up to the plate. I wrap my hands around the bat and take a deep breath. I know that this hit can win the game for us. But, I'm not nervous because baseball is my game, and I love it.

4. A. _____   Spaghetti is my favorite food. It is delicious.

   B. _____   "We had spaghetti two nights ago!" my brother whines. "It's my favorite," I reply. "I can't get enough of the juicy meatballs and the sweet tomato sauce. Come on. Can we ask Mom to make it again tonight?" I beg him. Spaghetti is definitely my favorite food!

Terrific Beginnings, Part One

Good authors grab the reader's attention from the start. A **terrific beginning** will make the reader want to continue reading.

Think about a time when you or someone you know found something unexpected. Write a terrific beginning for your story using action or dialogue. Use words from the word bank to help.

Action and Dialogue Word Bank		
amazed	confused	demanded
discovered	exclaimed	explored
gasped	investigated	replied

_____

_____

_____

_____

_____

_____

_____

_____

_____

_____

_____

_____

_____

_____

Name _____ Date _____

Terrific Beginnings, Part One

Good authors grab the reader's attention from the start. A **terrific beginning** will make the reader want to continue reading.

Think about a special day in your life. Tell a story about what happened on that day. Write a beginning using each terrific beginning technique: action and dialogue.

Terrific Beginning: Action

_____

_____

_____

_____

_____

_____

_____

_____

Terrific Beginning: Dialogue

_____

_____

_____

_____

_____

_____

_____

_____

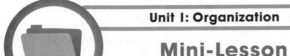

Mini-Lesson

Terrific Beginnings, Part Two

Good authors use a variety of opening strategies to capture the reader's attention. This lesson will introduce two additional strategies for writing terrific beginnings.

Mini-Lesson:

- Tell students that they will learn two ways to write a terrific beginning: using onomatopoeia and using the five senses.

- If students are not familiar with onomatopoeia, begin with a quick review of sound words. Write on the board a list of words such as *boom*, *ring*, *crash*, *hiss*, *squeak*, and *pop*. Explain to students that they can grab the reader's attention by including these words in their terrific beginnings.

- Review the five senses: hearing, sight, touch, taste, and smell. Write these words on the board. Tell students that thinking about the senses will help them write terrific beginnings.

- Model writing a terrific beginning using each strategy. Use the examples or have students help you write new beginnings.

Boring Beginning: Costume parties are fun.

Onomatopoeia: "Cock-a-doodle-do!" The cry of the rooster could be heard throughout the room. He took a deep breath, shook his feathers, and smiled. Everyone giggled at the sight of Gabriel dressed as a rooster. The costume party was off to a great start.

The Five Senses: As I entered the crowded room, I noticed the sparkling orange and white lights hanging from the ceiling. The smell of popcorn filled the air. I could see action superheroes, firefighters, and princesses dancing to the lively music. Everyone was laughing and having a good time. The costume party was a success!

Terrific Beginnings, Part Two

Good authors grab the reader's attention from the start. A **terrific beginning** will make the reader want to continue reading.

Read each pair of story beginnings. Decide which beginnings use onomatopoeia or the five senses. Write *yes* if the beginning is terrific. Write *no* if the beginning is not terrific.

1. A. _____ Crash! The Niagara River plunges over a rock cliff. More than 600,000 gallons of water pour down Horseshoe Falls every second.

   B. _____ The Niagara River dumps a lot of water over Horseshoe Falls.

2. A. _____ My mom said that I can get a pet. I hope that she will let me get a parrot instead of a kitten.

   B. _____ The door slammed behind us as we entered the animal shelter. My body tingled all over when I heard the tiny creatures. Then, I spotted her. Her soft brown eyes made my heart melt. Now, I need to convince my mom that a parrot would make an excellent pet.

3. A. _____ Buzz, buzz. The honeybee zooms from one flower to the next. Producing honey is hard work! This amazing insect can visit up to 100 flowers on each trip. Now, I understand what it means to be as busy as a bee!

   B. _____ Honeybees are very active. They are amazing.

4. A. _____ My heart starts to pound loudly in my chest. Beads of sweat trickle down my forehead. I can feel the creepy spider's dark eyes staring at me from across the room. I know that it can sense my fear.

   B. _____ I think that spiders are creepy. I am afraid of them.

Terrific Beginnings, Part Two

Good authors grab the reader's attention from the start. A **terrific beginning** will make the reader want to continue reading.

Imagine that you woke up one morning and were 10 feet (3 meters) tall. What would you do if you were that tall? Write a terrific beginning for your story using onomatopoeia (sound words) or the five senses (hearing, sight, touch, taste, and smell). Use words from the word bank to help.

Onomatopoeia Word Bank		Five Senses Word Bank	
bang	crash	appeared	felt
honk	giggle	looked	heard
screech	sigh	saw	touched

_____

_____

_____

_____

_____

_____

_____

_____

_____

_____

_____

_____

_____

_____

_____

Terrific Beginnings, Part Two

Good authors grab the reader's attention from the start. A **terrific beginning** will make the reader want to continue reading.

Stormy days are bound to happen. Do you like or dislike them? Why? Tell about a stormy day that you remember by writing two terrific beginnings. Use onomatopoeia (sound words) to write one terrific beginning. Use the five senses (hearing, sight, touch, taste, and smell) to write another terrific beginning.

Terrific Beginning: Onomatopoeia

_____

_____

_____

_____

_____

_____

Terrific Beginning: The Five Senses

_____

_____

_____

_____

_____

_____

_____

Mini-Lesson

Satisfying Endings, Part One

Many students have difficulty writing conclusions. They often focus on the details that they are writing and forget to include a cohesive ending. The following strategies will help students create satisfying endings.

Mini-Lesson:

- Ask students how they would feel if they were reading a story and the last two pages were missing.

- Discuss the importance of story endings. Tell students that in addition to a terrific beginning, a story must have a satisfying ending to make it feel complete. Write the sentences on the board:

  It was fun.   It was all a dream!   The end.   That's all.

- Ask students if they would be satisfied if their favorite stories ended this way.

- Tell students to imagine writing a story about a boy named Conner. Write the story information on the board:

  Character
  Conner is 10 years old. He loves to draw and paint.

  Problem
  Conner would like to learn how to create other types of art.

  Solution
  He asks his art teacher to help him. She teaches Conner how to make sculptures using items from the recycling bin.

- Introduce two strategies for creating satisfying endings. Use the examples or have students help you write new endings based on these strategies.

Summarizing the Main Idea:
Learning to create with recycled items was more fun than I could have hoped for! It has helped me understand that I can create artwork from many things.

Hinting at What Is to Come:
Learning to sculpt was more fun than I could have hoped for! Now, I want my art teacher to show me how to make pottery.

Connection: Connect this lesson to Terrific Beginnings, Part One. The mini-lessons and activities for both skills can be linked to show students how beginnings and endings can complement each other.

Satisfying Endings, Part One

Good authors use satisfying endings to make what they are writing feel complete. A **satisfying ending** can be either positive or negative, but it should create a strong finish.

Read each pair of story endings. Decide which ending is satisfying. Write *yes* if the ending is satisfying. Write *no* if the ending is not satisfying.

1. A. _____ Finally, our dull Sunday evening had become exciting. We didn't know when the power would come back on, but reading my homework assignment with a flashlight had been fun. I turned off the flashlight and went to sleep.

   B. _____ Sunday evening was over. Good-bye.

2. A. _____ We all got in our car. The end.

   B. _____ My hair and clothes were still wet as we started the long drive home. I wrapped myself in a towel, closed my eyes, and thought about the great fun we all had at the water park.

3. A. _____ Then, we had spaghetti for dinner. That's all.

   B. _____ Then, Mom surprised me with my favorite meal, spaghetti. My brother groaned a little, but I thought that it was the perfect ending to a terrific day.

4. A. _____ I am already thinking about my next baseball game. I hope that our team can win four in a row!

   B. _____ I had a great time playing baseball last night. Then, I went home.

Satisfying Endings, Part One

Good authors use satisfying endings to make what they are writing feel complete. A **satisfying ending** can be either positive or negative, but it should create a strong finish.

Read the story details. Write a satisfying ending to the story by either summarizing the main idea or hinting at what is to come.

Character

Ansley is 10 years old. She is hardworking but not athletic.

Problem

Ansley wants to learn how to play soccer.

Solution

She practices with her dad every day until she tries out for the school soccer team. She makes the team.

Satisfying Ending

_____

_____

_____

_____

_____

_____

_____

_____

_____

_____

Satisfying Endings, Part One

Good authors use satisfying endings to make what they are writing feel complete. A **satisfying ending** can be either positive or negative, but it should create a strong finish.

Read the story details. Write one ending by summarizing the main idea and another ending by hinting at what is to come.

Character

Barbara is nine years old. Her parents give her a weekly allowance of five dollars for doing her chores.

Problem

Barbara wants to buy a new video game system.

Solution

She saves her weekly allowance to purchase the video game system. After six months, she has saved enough to buy it.

Satisfying Ending: Summarizing the Main Idea

_____

_____

_____

_____

Satisfying Ending: Hinting at What Is to Come

_____

_____

_____

_____

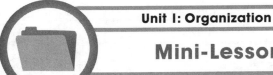
Good authors use a variety of endings in their writing. This lesson introduces two additional strategies for writing satisfying endings.

Mini-Lesson:

- Remind students that a satisfying ending makes writing feel complete. Endings such as "The End" or "Then, I woke up" can leave the reader wanting more.

- Tell students to imagine that they are writing a story about two friends named Lourdes and Sandra. Write the story information on the board:

Characters

Lourdes and Sandra are nine years old. They are best friends, and they love animals.

Problem

Lourdes's parents take them to the petting zoo. Lourdes and Sandra wonder if they will have any adventures there.

Solution

While Sandra is feeding a baby camel, a goat eats her hat! Their time at the petting zoo becomes their favorite adventure together.

- Introduce the two strategies for writing a satisfying ending: asking a question and learning a lesson. Use the examples or have students help you write new endings based on these strategies.

Asking a Question: Lourdes and Sandra still giggle when they tell the story of their adventure at the petting zoo. They wonder, What will our next adventure bring?

Learning a Lesson: Sandra was able to get away just in time. They enjoyed their adventure at the petting zoo but promised each other that they would be more careful the next time they were near a goat.

Connection: Connect this lesson to Terrific Beginnings, Part Two. The mini-lessons and activities for both skills can be linked to show students how beginnings and endings can complement each other.

Satisfying Endings, Part Two

The ending of a story is an author's last chance to make a good impression on the reader. A **satisfying ending** can be either positive or negative, but it should give the story a strong finish.

Read each pair of story endings. Write *yes* if the ending is satisfying. Write *no* if the ending is not satisfying.

1. A. _____ Engineers try to control the millions of gallons of water per minute flowing over Horseshoe Falls. But, no one has been able to stop the flow for 12,000 years. Will scientists ever find a way?

   B. _____ The water at Horseshoe Falls keeps flowing. The end.

2. A. _____ I did not get the parrot that I wanted. That's all!

   B. _____ Even though I did not get the parrot that I had hoped for, I learned a lesson. The next time I ask for a pet, I will ask for one that sleeps at night and is not so noisy!

3. A. _____ Honeybees are hard workers. Now that I know how helpful they are to the environment, I will not disturb them as they buzz around my garden. I hope that they won't disturb me again, either!

   B. _____ Honeybees help our environment. That's it.

4. A. _____ I finally understand that most spiders are not dangerous, so I am not as scared as I was that day. But, I still would not want to be alone in a room with a creepy, crawly spider! Would you?

   B. _____ Spiders are scary. I don't like them.

Satisfying Endings, Part Two

The ending of a story is an author's last chance to make a good impression on the reader. A **satisfying ending** can be either positive or negative, but it should give the story a strong finish.

Read the story details. Write a satisfying ending to the story by asking a question or having the characters learn a lesson.

Characters

Scotty is a golden retriever who loves to play fetch.
Mark is Scotty's owner.

Problem

Scotty gets lost in the park while playing fetch with Mark.

Solution

Mark finally finds Scotty waiting for him by the swings.

Satisfying Ending

_____

_____

_____

_____

_____

_____

_____

_____

_____

_____

_____

_____

_____

Satisfying Endings, Part Two

The ending of a story is an author's last chance to make a good impression on the reader. A **satisfying ending** can be either positive or negative, but it should give the story a strong finish.

Read the story details. Write two satisfying endings to the story. One ending should ask a question. In the other ending, the characters should learn a lesson.

Characters

Your teacher
You

Problem

Your teacher leaves you in charge of his students. At first, the students misbehave.

Solution

Then, the students begin to follow the rules.

Satisfying Ending: Asking a Question

_____

_____

_____

_____

_____

Satisfying Ending: Learning a Lesson

_____

_____

_____

_____

_____

_____

Mini-Lesson

Using Time-Order Words

Transitional devices are used in writing to connect ideas. They help carry the reader from one sentence to another. Authors use transitional words to organize their thoughts and present them in a unified manner. Time-order words in particular indicate that another step or event is about to be presented.

Time-Order Words and Phrases				
after	after a few hours	at this point	eventually	finally
first, second, etc.	immediately	last	later	meanwhile
next	now	previously	soon	then

Mini-Lesson:

- Using the examples, write a list of time-order words on chart paper, but do not show it to students.

- Write the passage on the board:

  Take out your reading book. Turn to page 45. Take out a sheet of paper. Write your heading on your paper. Complete questions 1–10. Review your work. Read silently.

- Ask students if these directions are easy to follow. Then, ask how they can make the directions easier to understand and make them sound better. Guide them into discussing the order in which the directions should be followed. Often, students use transitional words to explain the steps. Use this opportunity to present time-order words.

- Tell students that certain words indicate the order of steps or events that occur.

- Reveal the list of time-order words. Have students select words from the list that will make your directions easier to follow.

- Rewrite the paragraph using these transitional words. Read it aloud. Emphasize the flow of the new paragraph and how these new words have tied the steps together.

 Extension

In a pocket chart, use sentence strips to rewrite the above passage. Write time-order words on index cards and give them to several students. Have students revise the directions by placing the index cards in appropriate spaces in the chart.

Using Time-Order Words

Time-order words help authors organize their thoughts. These words can connect one sentence to the next. Time-order words help the reader understand the order of events.

Examples: *eventually, finally, first, last, next, now, shortly after, soon, then*

Read the paragraph. Underline the time-order words or phrases. Then, write the words.

Growing a Sunflower

Did you know that you can plant a sunflower seed inside a cup? It is simple and fun! First, gather the following materials: a clear, plastic cup; a wet paper towel; and a sunflower seed. Next, place the paper towel inside the cup. At this point, make sure that the paper towel covers the entire inside of the cup. Place the seed on the paper towel and fold the paper towel over the seed. Then, place the cup near a window with a lot of sunlight shining through. If your plant does not get enough sunlight, it will not be able to grow. It will take three weeks for your seed to sprout. Meanwhile, you can record any changes that you observe. Finally, you will be able to see your sunflower flourish!

1. _____
2. _____
3. _____
4. _____
5. _____
6. _____

 Extra: Reread the steps. Try to follow the directions without the time-order words. Do you think that planting the seed would be easier or more difficult without these words? Why?

Using Time-Order Words

Time-order words help authors organize their thoughts. These words can connect one sentence to the next. Time-order words help the reader understand the order of events.

Examples: *eventually, finally, first, last, next, now, shortly after, soon, then*

Read the paragraph. The time-order words have been left out. On each line, write a time-order word to complete each sentence.

Monday mornings are always hectic for me. Mom and Dad have a lot for me to do before I can leave for school. _____ , I have to take a warm shower. This always helps me wake up and get ready for the day ahead. _____ , I put on my clothes. This part is easy because I wear my school uniform each day. _____ , I have to make my bed. I can't even think about having breakfast until I make my bed. _____ , I have to wake my little brother. He gets to sleep later than I do. I try to wake him slowly. _____ , I whisper his name. _____ , I give him a gentle push. If that doesn't work, I have no choice but to yell, "Tommy, get up!" That usually does the trick. _____ my stomach starts growling, so I eat a bowl of cereal. On Monday mornings, we have no time for fluffy pancakes. I _____ brush my teeth and comb my hair. I can _____ head off to school!

Using Time-Order Words

Time-order words help authors organize their thoughts. These words can connect one sentence to the next. Time-order words help the reader understand the order of events.

Examples: *eventually, finally, first, last, next, now, shortly after, soon, then*

Imagine that someone has asked you for the directions to make your favorite sandwich. Help them by writing the steps. Use at least six time-order words.

How to Make My Favorite _____ Sandwich

_____

_____

_____

_____

_____

_____

_____

_____

_____

_____

_____

_____

_____

_____

Mini-Lesson

Writing to Compare and Contrast

The compare-and-contrast text structure requires authors to explain how two or more things are alike and different. Authors must analyze the objects or events they are writing about and decide how to present the information. Students can use the following words and phrases to signal similarities and differences in their writing.

Words and Phrases That Compare		Words and Phrases That Contrast	
also	as	although	as opposed to
both	have in common	but	even though
in the same way	just as	however	nevertheless
like	same	on the contrary	on the other hand
similar	too	unlike	while

Mini-Lesson:

- Ask students about having a pet. Tell them that if they were thinking of getting a cat or a dog, comparing the two pets would help them make the decision.

- Introduce the graphic organizer (page 43). Draw it on the board. Tell students that you will compare and contrast cats and dogs. Tell students that understanding how the pets are alike and different may help them choose one.

- List the two pets to compare and contrast on the chart.

- Have students help you list the attributes that are alike.

- Have students indicate some differences between cats and dogs. List them on the chart.

- Introduce the key words and phrases used to compare and contrast objects. Show students how to use these words. For example, explain that both animals can live indoors. However, some dogs can grow very large and cats are more standard in size.

- Use these words to create two paragraphs on the board. One paragraph should explain the similarities. The other should explain the differences. Have students come to the board and circle the key words that signal the similarities and differences.

- Ask students which pet they would choose based on the comparison.

Objects to Compare

Cats and Dogs

How They Are Alike
(Key Words: *both, common, like, same*)

1. They have fur.
2. They require shots and exams.
3. They can be house-trained.

How They Are Different
(Key Words: *but, different, however, unlike*)

Cats
1. Meow
2. Need less exercise
3. Use a litter box

Dogs
1. Bark
2. Need more exercise
3. Use the bathroom outdoors

Name _____ Date _____

Writing to Compare and Contrast

When authors **compare and contrast** two objects or ideas, they tell how the objects are alike and how they are different.

Think about how you and your friends are similar and how you are different. Choose one friend to compare and contrast with yourself. Complete the story frame.

My friend's name is _____ .

We have many things in common. For example, we both _____

_____ . We also

_____

_____ .

Another thing that we have in common is _____

_____ .

My friend and I are also different in several ways. _____

likes to _____ ,

but I like to _____ .

_____ thinks _____

_____ .

However, I think _____

_____ .

I enjoy _____

_____ .

On the other hand, my friend enjoys _____ .

Our likes and dislikes help keep our friendship strong!

(!) **Extra:** Circle the compare and contrast key words in the story frame.

Name _____   Date _____

Writing to Compare and Contrast

When authors **compare and contrast** two objects or ideas, they tell how the objects are alike and how they are different.

Think about two places that you would like to visit. Compare and contrast these two places to help you decide which one you would prefer to visit. Then, use the flowchart to help you write two paragraphs on another sheet of paper. In the paragraphs, compare and contrast the places that you would like to visit.

Two Places I Want to Visit: _____ and _____

How They Are Alike
(Key Words: *both, common, like, same*)

How They Are Different
(Key Words: *but, different, however, unlike*)

1. _____
_____
_____
2. _____
_____
_____
3. _____
_____
_____
4. _____
_____
_____

1. _____
_____
_____
2. _____
_____
_____
3. _____
_____
_____
4. _____
_____
_____

1. _____
_____
_____
2. _____
_____
_____
3. _____
_____
_____
4. _____
_____
_____

Name _____   Date _____

Writing to Compare and Contrast

When authors **compare and contrast** two objects or ideas, they tell how the objects are alike and how they are different.

Think about two objects, events, or places to compare and contrast. Fill in the chart with the details. Then, use the flowchart to help you write two paragraphs on another sheet of paper. In the paragraphs, compare and contrast the topic.

Topic: _____ and _____

How They Are Alike
(Key Words: *both, common, like, same*)

1. _____
   _____
   _____
2. _____
   _____
   _____
3. _____
   _____
   _____
4. _____
   _____
   _____

How They Are Different
(Key Words: *but, different, however, unlike*)

1. _____
   _____
   _____
2. _____
   _____
   _____
3. _____
   _____
   _____
4. _____
   _____
   _____

1. _____
   _____
   _____
2. _____
   _____
   _____
3. _____
   _____
   _____
4. _____
   _____
   _____

Informative Writing

Mini-Lesson

Authors use informative, or expository, writing to express their ideas and opinions to the reader. In this lesson, students will use background knowledge to expand on a topic and provide information.

Mini-Lesson:

- Ask students what they want to be when they grow up. Discuss why the careers appeal to them. Share some careers that you considered when you were a child.

- Tell students that they will write essays explaining why they like particular careers.

- Model how to organize ideas by creating a graphic organizer on the board. (See the example below.) Tell students that your essay will be about wanting to become a teacher (or another career). Write the topic on your chart.

- Explain to students that you will begin by writing two reasons why you thought that you would like this career. Model this portion by writing your first reason. Then, write an example and details to support the reason.

- Have students offer a second reason why someone might want to be a teacher. Fill in reason two, a supporting example, and details on the chart.

- Explain to students how this chart helped you plan your writing and how it can help them create a plan for writing.

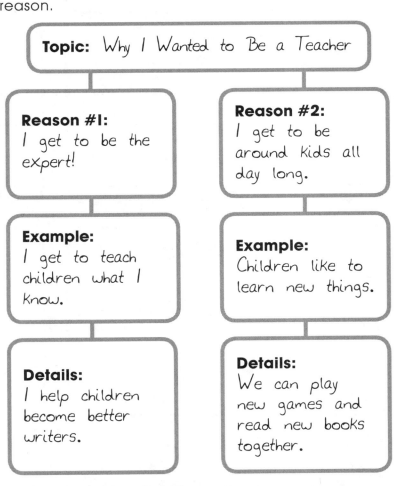

Topic: Why I Wanted to Be a Teacher

Reason #1: I get to be the expert!

Reason #2: I get to be around kids all day long.

Example: I get to teach children what I know.

Example: Children like to learn new things.

Details: I help children become better writers.

Details: We can play new games and read new books together.

Name _____   Date _____

Informative Writing

When **writing to inform**, authors can use personal ideas and feelings to explain different topics.

Many students love the summer. Think about the summer and why this time of year is special. Complete the chart with examples and details that support the two reasons.

Topic: *Summer*

Reason #1: There is no school.

Example:
_____
_____
_____
_____
_____

Details:
_____
_____
_____
_____

Reason #2: The weather is warm.

Example:
_____
_____
_____
_____
_____

Details:
_____
_____
_____
_____

Name _____ Date _____

Informative Writing

When **writing to inform**, authors can use personal ideas and feelings to explain different topics.

Everyone has a favorite place. Explain why your favorite place is special to you. Complete the chart to express your ideas and feelings on the topic.

Topic: My Favorite Place Is _____ .

Reason #1: I like this place because
_____
_____
_____ .

Reason #2: I like this place because
_____
_____
_____ .

Example:
_____
_____
_____

Example:
_____
_____
_____

Details:
_____
_____
_____
_____
_____

Details:
_____
_____
_____
_____
_____

Name _____   Date _____

Informative Writing

When **writing to inform**, authors can use personal ideas and feelings to explain different topics.

Books are special to many people. Think about your favorite book and why it is your favorite. Complete the chart to express your ideas and feelings on the topic.

Topic: _____

Reason #1:	**Reason #2:**
_____ _____ _____ _____ .	_____ _____ _____ _____ .
Example:	**Example:**
_____ _____ _____	_____ _____ _____
Details:	**Details:**
_____ _____ _____	_____ _____ _____

 Extra: On another sheet of paper, write an essay about your favorite book. Use the chart to help you explain why it is your favorite book.

Writing to Persuade

Mini-Lesson

In persuasive writing, the author expresses an opinion and tries to convince the reader to agree and take action on it. Students will practice writing persuasively by using reasons and supporting details.

Examples:

No Supporting Details: I think that I deserve a bigger allowance. I think that you should give me $4 instead of $2. Please, please, please give me a bigger allowance.

Supporting Details: I think that I deserve a bigger allowance. You should double my allowance because I help with the chores, I always keep my room neat and clean, and I have improved my grades in school.

Mini-Lesson:

- Explain to students that when writing to persuade, the author should answer *what*, *who*, and *why*.

- Write the following on the board: *What* is your opinion on the topic? ("I deserve a bigger allowance.") *Who* is your reader? (My parents.) *Why* do you think others should agree with your opinion? ("I help with the chores," etc.)

- Brainstorm a list of possible classroom rules that students wish could be implemented. Rules could include: gum chewing is allowed on Fridays, students get free time every morning, etc. Model the planning of a persuasive essay using the most popular rule(s) suggested. Collaboratively select the *what* (rule to be implemented), *who* (the teacher), and *why* (students' rationale for rule choice).

- Pair students. Have each pair practice planning a persuasive essay on a different topic and for a different audience. Partners must list the *what*, *who*, and *why* for their persuasive essays. Have partners share and discuss their ideas with the class.

- Apply the graphic organizer on page 54 to any persuasive writing.

Book List
Examples of *what*, *who*, and *why* can be found in *Earrings!* and *The True Story of the 3 Little Pigs*.

Name _____ Date _____

Writing to Persuade

When **writing to persuade**, the author wants the reader to agree with his opinion. Before writing, answer the questions:

- *What* is your opinion?

- *Whom* are you trying to convince?

- *Why* do you think that others should agree with your opinion?

Imagine that your teacher has decided to rearrange students' desks. Should students be allowed to choose where they sit in class? Use the graphic organizer to help you plan your persuasive paragraph.

What is your opinion on the topic?

_____

_____

_____

_____

Whom are you trying to persuade?

_____

_____

_____

_____

Why do you think that others should agree with your opinion? List three reasons to support your opinion.

1. _____

_____

2. _____

_____

3. _____

_____

 Extra: On another sheet of paper, use your notes to help you write a five-sentence persuasive paragraph.

Name _____ Date _____

Writing to Persuade

When **writing to persuade**, the author wants the reader to agree with his opinion. Before writing, answer the questions:

- *What* is your opinion?

- *Whom* are you trying to convince?

- *Why* do you think that others should agree with your opinion?

Imagine that your teacher is thinking about taking the class on a field trip to a farm. But, you would rather go to a fire station. Think of reasons why the fire station would be a better place to go. Use the graphic organizer to help you plan your persuasive essay.

What is your opinion on the topic?

_____

_____

_____

Whom are you trying to persuade?

_____

_____

_____

Why do you think that others should agree with your opinion? List two reasons to support your opinion.

1. _____

2. _____

For each reason, add supporting details to help convince the reader that your reasons are important.

1. _____

_____

2. _____

_____

 Extra: On another sheet of paper, use your notes to help you write a five-sentence persuasive paragraph.

Writing to Persuade

When **writing to persuade**, the author wants the reader to agree with his opinion and possibly take action. Before writing, answer the questions:

- *What* is your opinion?

- *Whom* are you trying to convince?

- *Why* do you think that others should agree with your opinion?

Choose a topic. Use the graphic organizer to help you plan a persuasive essay.

What is your opinion on the topic?

_____

_____

_____

Whom are you trying to persuade?

_____

_____

_____

Why do you think that others should agree with your opinion? List three reasons to support your opinion.

1. _____

2. _____

3. _____

To convince the reader, add supporting details for each reason.

1. _____

2. _____

3. _____

 Extra: On another sheet of paper, use your notes to help you write a five-paragraph persuasive essay. Include three reasons, in addition to introductory and concluding paragraphs.

Writing Poetry: Bio Poems

Mini-Lesson

Writing poetry gives students opportunities to explore and use language in new ways. A bio poem teaches students to focus on selecting specific, descriptive words. It also requires students to think critically about the subject and express themselves using a specific format.

Mini-Lesson:

- Begin a discussion on the characteristics of heroes. Ask students to tell about some of their heroes. Create a list on the board. Guide students toward famous heroes, such as historic figures, so that all students will know of the people being discussed.

- Tell students that they will each write a bio poem. Tell them that a bio poem uses a specific format to describe a person.

- Copy the format for a bio poem on the board. (See the example below). Fill in the first and last names of the hero.

- Have students help you complete the poem. Guide students into selecting advanced vocabulary words. For example, if students believe that the hero feels happy, ask them why they think that he is happy. Then, ask them to think of a more specific word to describe this feeling. Words like *overjoyed* and *excited* may be appropriate choices.

Bio Poem Format:	Example:
Line 1: First name (centered)	Helen
Line 2: Three adjectives to describe the person	Inspiring, determined, tenacious
Line 3: He/she feels . . .	She feels frustrated and isolated.
Line 4: He/she wants . . .	She wants guidance and direction.
Line 5: He/she loves . . .	She loves to acquire knowledge.
Line 6: He/she gives . . .	She gives her strength and trust.
Line 7: He/she wonders . . .	She wonders about tomorrow.
Line 8: Last name (centered)	Keller

Name _____ Date _____

Writing Poetry

In **poetry**, authors use words in special ways to tell stories or to describe feelings or ideas. Poems can be written about any subject and can take a variety of forms. A bio poem describes a person and uses a specific format.

Imagine that someone is describing you. Follow the format to write a bio poem about yourself. Choose words that describe your personality.

_____

First name

_____

Three adjectives to describe myself

He/she feels _____ .

(up to two items)

He/she wants _____ .

(up to three items)

He/she loves _____ .

(up to three items)

He/she gives _____ .

(up to three items)

He/she wonders _____ .

(up to two items)

_____

Last name

Writing Poetry

In **poetry**, writers use words in special ways to tell stories or to describe feelings or ideas. Poems can be written about any subject and can take a variety of forms. A bio poem describes a person and uses a specific format.

Follow the format to write a bio poem about someone that you know well. Choose words that describe this person's personality.

_____
First name

_____
Three adjectives to describe the person

He/she feels _____ .

(up to two items)

He/she laughs at _____ .

(up to two items)

He/she loves _____ .

(up to three items)

He/she understands _____ .

(up to three items)

He/she fears _____ .

(up to three items)

He/she gives _____ .

(up to three items)

He/she would like to see _____ .

(up to two items)

_____
Last name

Writing Poetry

In **poetry**, authors use words in special ways to tell stories or to describe feelings or ideas. Poems can be written about any subject and can take a variety of forms. A bio poem describes a person and uses a specific format.

Think of your favorite book character. Follow the format to write a bio poem about that character. Choose the pronoun *he, she,* or *it* to write in each short blank. Complete each line with words to describe the character's personality.

_____

First name

_____

Three adjectives to describe the character

_____ feels _____ .

(up to two items)

_____ wants _____ .

(up to three items)

_____ loves _____ .

(up to three items)

_____ understands _____ .

(up to three items)

_____ fears _____ .

(up to three items)

_____ gives _____ .

(up to three items)

_____ wonders _____ .

(up to two items)

_____

Last name

Writing a Friendly Letter

Mini-Lesson

A friendly letter is a form of communication between people who usually know each other well. It is informal. A friendly letter usually includes personal information about the sender and asks questions of the recipient. Writing a friendly letter can help students improve their writing skills. It reinforces skills such as paragraph structure, proper conventions, and awareness of audience.

Mini-Lesson:

- Begin with a short discussion about friends and classmates who have moved to other towns. Explain that letter writing helps people stay in touch when they have moved away.

- Tell students that the class will write a friendly letter to a classmate who has moved.

- Write the format for a friendly letter on the board. Review it with the class.

  heading (writer's address and date)
  greeting (Dear _____,)
  body (content)
  closing (Your friends,)
  signature (name of sender)

- Have students brainstorm topics and create a web (see page 60) on the board with information that could be included in the letter.

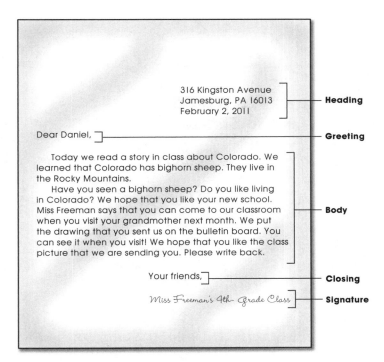

316 Kingston Avenue
Jamesburg, PA 16013
February 2, 2011 — **Heading**

Dear Daniel, — **Greeting**

Today we read a story in class about Colorado. We learned that Colorado has bighorn sheep. They live in the Rocky Mountains.
    Have you seen a bighorn sheep? Do you like living in Colorado? We hope that you like your new school. Miss Freeman says that you can come to our classroom when you visit your grandmother next month. We put the drawing that you sent us on the bulletin board. You can see it when you visit! We hope that you like the class picture that we are sending you. Please write back. — **Body**

Your friends, — **Closing**

Miss Freeman's 4th Grade Class — **Signature**

- Model using the web to write the friendly letter. Refer to the format as you write.

- To reinforce writing skills, think aloud as you write. For example, say, "I told Daniel what we are learning in class. Now, I will start a new paragraph because I am writing about a new topic. I must be sure to indent the new paragraph."

- When the letter is complete, read it aloud and model self-editing. For example, as you read the letter, say, "I just noticed that I forgot to add a comma after Daniel's name. I will add it now. It is important to reread our writing at the end and catch our own mistakes!"

Friendly Letter to

Daniel

News We Would Like to Share

1. What we are studying
2. We put your drawing on the board.
3. We are sending a picture.

Questions We Would Like to Ask

1. Have you seen bighorn sheep?
2. Do you like Colorado?
3. Will you visit our class?

Book List

Examples of letter writing can be found in _Dear Mr. Blueberry, Dear Mr. Henshaw,_ and _Mailing May._

Writing a Friendly Letter

A friendly letter is one method of communication between people who know each other well. A friendly letter has five parts: the **heading**, the **greeting**, the **body**, the **closing**, and the **signature**.

Amad has written a friendly letter to his friend Kenneth. The following is the body of his letter. Fill in the blanks with the missing parts of the letter. Label each part of the friendly letter.

_____   _____

_____

_____

_____ ,   _____

    Summer camp is awesome! Every day at Camp Walden is an adventure. I can't believe I've been here for a whole week. I thought I would be homesick, but I love it here. The camp counselors are always happy, and the cabins have bunk beds.

    We have lots of activities, and we're pretty busy. On Monday, we split into teams and ran relay races. My team came in third place! On Tuesday, we went swimming in the lake. Some friends and I stayed near the edge and tried to do handstands and backflips into the water. On Wednesday before lights-out, we roasted marshmallows over a campfire. Next week, we will make s'mores! Have you ever had a s'more? My camp counselor told me it's made by squishing a roasted marshmallow and chocolate in between two graham crackers. It sounds delicious!

    I hope that you are enjoying your summer back home. Have you done anything special? Please write back.

_____ ,   _____

_____

Writing a Friendly Letter

A friendly letter is one method of communication between people who know each other well. A friendly letter has five parts: the **heading**, the **greeting**, the **body**, the **closing**, and the **signature**.

Think about a friend who is not in your class this year. Write a letter to your friend. Use this format for the body:

First paragraph: Tell your friend two things about your class.

Second paragraph: Tell your friend two new things about your life at home.

Third paragraph: Ask your friend two questions.

_____

_____

_____

Dear _____ ,

_____

_____

_____

_____

_____

_____

Your friend,

_____

Writing a Friendly Letter

A friendly letter is one method of communication between people who know each other well. A friendly letter has five parts: the **heading**, the **greeting**, the **body**, the **closing**, and the **signature**.

Write a friendly letter to a teacher you once had. Use the web to plan your letter. Select three topics to include in your letter. Then, list three details for each topic.

Use the web to help you write a friendly letter on another sheet of paper.

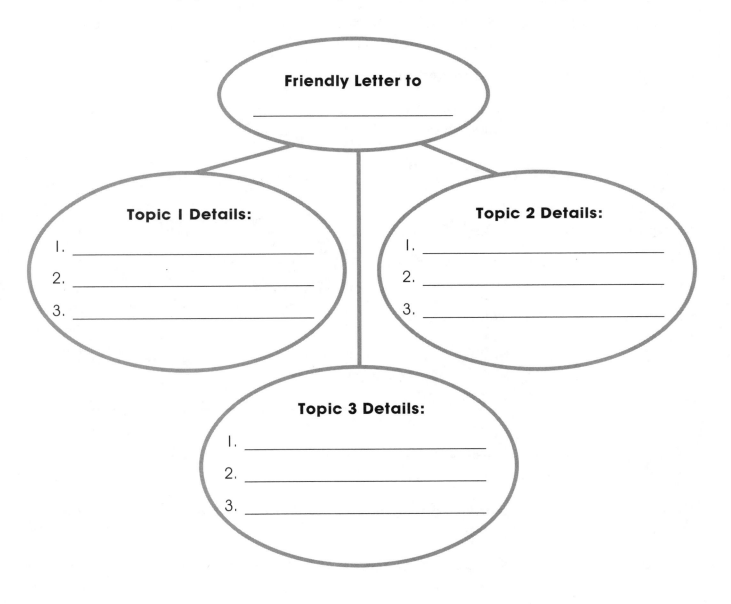

Friendly Letter to

_____

Topic 1 Details:

1. _____
2. _____
3. _____

Topic 2 Details:

1. _____
2. _____
3. _____

Topic 3 Details:

1. _____
2. _____
3. _____

A business letter is a formal method of communication. Students can write business letters to communicate with local businesses, community members, private organizations, and public agencies.

Mini-Lesson:

- Begin with a short discussion about the importance of protecting the environment.

- Tell students that they will write a business letter to request information on additional ways to protect the planet.

- Re-create the business letter format on the board. The body of the letter can be used as a sample. But, students should help you write the final letter.

- Review the six parts of a business letter:

  heading (sender's address and date)
  inside address (recipient's name and address)
  greeting (Dear _____:)
  body (content)
  closing (Sincerely,)
  signature (name of sender)

- Bring special attention to the block format and the use of the colon in the greeting.

- Have students help you write the body of the letter.

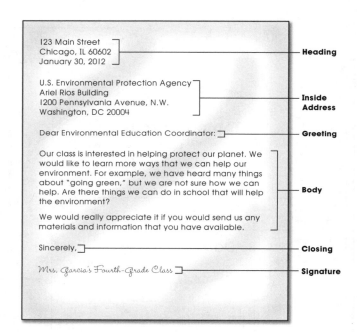

- 123 Main Street
  Chicago, IL 60602
  January 30, 2012 — **Heading**

- U.S. Environmental Protection Agency
  Ariel Rios Building
  1200 Pennsylvania Avenue, N.W.
  Washington, DC 20004 — **Inside Address**

- Dear Environmental Education Coordinator: — **Greeting**

- Our class is interested in helping protect our planet. We would like to learn more ways that we can help our environment. For example, we have heard many things about "going green," but we are not sure how we can help. Are there things we can do in school that will help the environment?

  We would really appreciate it if you would send us any materials and information that you have available. — **Body**

- Sincerely, — **Closing**

- *Mrs. Garcia's Fourth-Grade Class* — **Signature**

Extensions

- With the class, write a letter to a local organization to request information about a topic in which your students have shown interest.

- Teach students how to address an envelope. Mail the letter.

Writing a Business Letter

A business letter is a formal method of communication between individuals or groups who may not know each other well. A business letter has six parts: the **heading**, the **inside address**, the **greeting**, the **body**, the **closing**, and the **signature**.

This business letter is out of order. Cut out the parts of the letter. Glue them in the correct order on another sheet of paper.

Sincerely,

Mrs. Hurns
Palm Elementary School
456 Bobcat Way
Miami, FL 32986

Eva Davis
Eva Davis

123 Dade Pine Ct.
Miami, FL 33016
February 7, 2011

Dear Mrs. Hurns:

I would like to ask you to add a new food to the menu. I would especially like to have veggie pizzas as part of our school lunch.

The students in my fourth-grade class like the chicken, hamburgers, and spaghetti and meatballs that we eat for lunch, but we would like a meatless choice too. Veggie pizza can be made quickly and would not take up too much time. The cafeteria staff might be happy to make something new that everyone can enjoy. The ingredients in this meal are also part of a well-balanced diet. This will help us grow strong and healthy.

Thank you for taking the time to read my suggestion. I hope that you will think about it.

cut

 Extra: After you have glued the business letter in the correct order, label the six parts of the letter.

Writing a Business Letter

A business letter is a formal method of communication between individuals or groups who may not know each other well. A business letter has six parts: the **heading**, the **inside address**, the **greeting**, the **body**, the **closing**, and the **signature**.

Reading in a park is a great way to enjoy the outdoors. Complete the business letter to the director of a local park. Ask for permission to hold a class reading day at the park. Explain what you would like to do at the park and why you think that it is a great idea.

176 Candlewood Lane
Victoria, British Columbia V9B 2Z8
May 4, 2011

Mr. Alberto Perez
Parks and Community Services
490 Atkins Avenue
Victoria, British Columbia V9B 2Z8

Dear Mr. Perez:

_____

_____

_____

_____

_____

_____

_____

Sincerely,

_____

Writing a Business Letter

A business letter is a formal method of communication between individuals or groups who may not know each other well. A business letter has six parts: the **heading**, the **inside address**, the **greeting**, the **body**, the **closing**, and the **signature**.

Imagine that you bought a brand-new bicycle. The next day, the handlebars broke off. Write a letter to the bicycle company to explain what happened. Be sure to ask for new handlebars.

_____

_____

_____

_____

_____

_____ :

_____

_____

_____

_____

_____

_____ ,

_____

 Extra: Label the six parts of your business letter.

Mini-Lesson

Choosing a Topic

Authors often use their own experiences to generate writing topics. Students will practice using personal experiences to write interesting stories.

Mini-Lesson:

- Select an object that reminds you of a special memory. For example, bring in a checkerboard that reminds you of playing checkers with your grandfather.

- Show the object to students and explain its significance. Tell students that the object will be your inspiration for writing a story. Explain that authors write about what they know and that special memories can make excellent writing topics.

- Ask students to think of special memories with family members. Create a "Special Times with Family Members" web on the board. Discuss the feelings associated with these memories. Have each student select one memory to write about.

Grandpa's Checkerboard

My grandpa liked to sit in his blue chair beside a little table with a little drawer. He would let me open the drawer and take out his box of checkers. We would stack them in tall piles, and he would let me knock them down. When I was six, Grandpa asked, "Do you want me to show you how to play checkers?" He opened the checkerboard and gave me my first lesson. He even let me win! We played checkers almost every time that I visited him. Now, he lives in a big place with other older people. But, I still go see him and we play checkers. He still lets me win!

Extension

Have students select objects from home to share with classmates. Write a list of possible writing topics based on these objects.

Choosing a Topic

There are several ways to choose a writing **topic**. Authors can write about their own experiences.

Strong feelings help people remember special or important times. Complete the statements. Then, think about which experiences would make interesting writing topics.

I really enjoyed it when . . .

1. _____ .

2. _____ .

3. _____ .

I felt sad when . . .

1. _____ .

2. _____ .

3. _____ .

I felt excited when . . .

1. _____ .

2. _____ .

3. _____ .

Look at your responses. List three experiences that you can use as writing topics.

1. _____

2. _____

3. _____

Name _____   Date _____

Choosing a Topic

There are several ways to choose a writing **topic**. Authors can write about their own experiences.

Do you remember the first time that you rode a bike or the first time that you rode on a roller coaster? Fill in the web with examples of your experiences. These examples can lead to great stories.

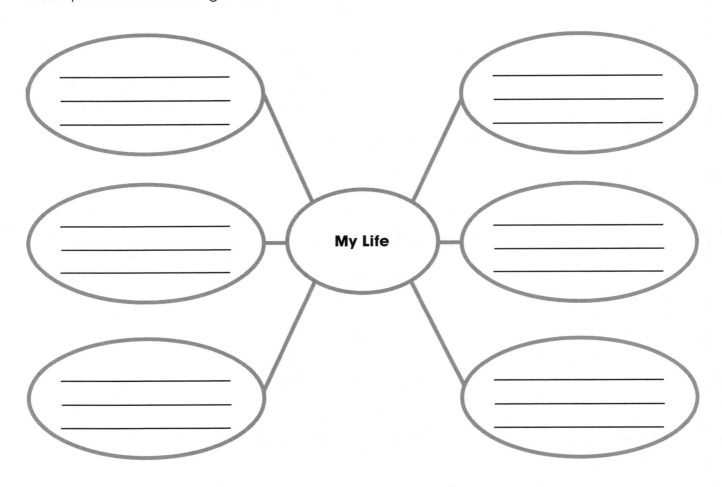

My Life

Look at the examples that you wrote on the web. List three experiences that you can write about.

1. _____

2. _____

3. _____

Choosing a Topic

There are several ways to choose a writing **topic**. Authors can write about their own experiences.

People have different talents and abilities. We are all experts on different things. List three things on which you consider yourself to be an expert. Explain why you are an expert on each.

Examples: I am an expert on photography. (I take my camera everywhere.)

I am an expert on my sister. (I know everything about her.)

1. _____

_____

_____

_____

2. _____

_____

_____

_____

3. _____

_____

_____

_____

 Extra: Look at the things that you listed. Choose one and use it as the topic of your next story.

Mini-Lesson   Focused Writing

Good authors focus on specific topics. Focused writing will help students narrow their topics and exclude extraneous information.

Focused Writing	Unfocused Writing
• Focuses on one specific topic or moment in time	• Tells a little bit about a lot of things
• Has details that relate to the main idea	• Wanders off topic
• Flows and is easy for the reader to follow	• Is often written in "list style"

Mini-Lesson:

• Reproduce the above chart on the board. Discuss focused and unfocused writing.

• Focused writing has a limited or specific subject. Begin by teaching students how to narrow writing topics. Students often choose large topics for their writing, such as "My Summer," "My Hobbies," or "All About Me." Tell students that you will demonstrate how to narrow the subject so that their writing is focused.

• Tell students that you will write about your family. Write "My Family" on the board. Explain that you have many relatives and could write a little bit about each of them, but that would make the topic too unfocused and too big.

• Think aloud about a person in your family who is special to you. Below the words "My Family," write the name of the relative (for example, "My Mother"). Then, explain that writing about your mother is still too unfocused.

• Think aloud about a special memory that you have of your mother (for example, a great day at the beach when you built a big sand castle together). Under the words "My Mother," write "A day at beach building sand castles with Mom."

• Explain to students that this would make your topic very specific and limited and would keep your writing focused. Have students select a family-based, focused topic to write about. Other possible topics include trips, friends, and holidays.

Focused Writing

Focused writing is about one specific, small topic. It tells a lot about one thing or moment.

Unfocused writing is about too many things. It tells a little bit about a lot of topics.

Read each short story. Write *yes* if the story is focused. Write *no* if it is unfocused.

_____ 1. My Friends

   I have a lot of friends who are important to me. My best friend is Jenny. She is smart and funny. We like to go to the movies. My other best friend is Josie. She likes to go biking with me, and we laugh a lot. I have two more good friends. Their names are Jill and Sasha. They are cool and fun to hang out with. Sometimes, I go to their houses or they come to mine. The kids in my class are also my friends, but we only see each other at school. I have a lot of great friends.

_____ 2. Race Day

   My fingers gripped the handlebars tightly as the starting gun went off. I began pedaling as fast as I could. It was my first bike race. I was excited, but nervous! The racers go around the track three times. Before I knew it, I was on my final lap. I was at the front of the pack! I saw another racer out of the corner of my eye. I knew that I had to pedal hard or I wouldn't get a medal. Gritting my teeth, I took a deep breath and pedaled faster than I ever had in my whole life. I could see the finish line and hear the crowd cheering. My heart pounded. I couldn't believe it! Everyone applauded as I crossed the finish line in first place.

_____ 3. My Trip to New York

   I went to New York with my family. The plane ride took a long time. I read a book to keep myself busy. When we got there, we checked into our hotel. Our room was on the 10th floor. Then, we went to the Statue of Liberty. Next, we went to the top of the Empire State Building. We ate lunch and bought some T-shirts. Two hours later, we went skating in Central Park. It was super cold, and I fell twice. Then, we went to dinner and went back to the hotel to go to sleep. The next day we did more stuff. It was cool visiting New York.

Focused Writing

Focused writing is about one specific, small topic. It tells a lot about one thing or moment. All of the details are important to the main idea. Focused writing does not have any extra, or unimportant, information. It stays on topic.

Unfocused writing is about too many things. It tells a little bit about a lot of topics. Some details are not important or have nothing to do with the main idea. This can make it hard for the reader to follow the story.

Read the story. The author goes off topic a few times and writes about things that have nothing to do with the main idea. Find details that are not related or not important and draw lines through them.

Test Day

It was the big day. Test Day! I was nervous as I walked into my class. I walked to my desk and sat down. Ben walked in, wearing a blue and white shirt. He has brown hair and freckles. I opened my backpack and took out my pencils. I wanted to be ready when Ms. Kincaid started the test. I had butterflies in my stomach. I tried to remember what my mother had told me at breakfast, "Relax and do your best. That is the most important thing." I had cereal for breakfast. My brother was there too, but he doesn't like cereal. The rest of my classmates arrived. Ms. Kincaid said hello to everyone and gave us a pep talk. She is a great teacher. She has worked hard to get us ready for Test Day. She is always in a good mood. My teacher last year wasn't like that. I want to be a teacher when I grow up, but I want to be like Ms. Kincaid. As Ms. Kincaid passed out the tests, I took out my lucky penny and put it in my pocket. My dad gave it to me when I was four. I put it in the pocket of my dress the night of my recital, right before I went on stage. I wore a beautiful pink dress with matching shoes that night. It was time! We began our test. I was super relieved that I knew most of the answers! My studying had paid off! A little later, Ms. Kincaid called time and asked Mary to help her collect the tests. Mary is new at our school. As I turned in my test, I breathed a sigh of relief. It was over! I had done it! I put my penny away and got ready for recess. Today we were going to play kickball, and I was excited because kickball is my favorite sport.

Focused Writing

Focused writing is about one specific, small topic. It tells a lot about one thing or moment. All of the details are important to the main idea. Focused writing does not have any extra, or unimportant, information. It stays on topic.

Unfocused writing is about too many things. It tells a little bit about a lot of topics. Some details are not important or have nothing to do with the main idea. This can make it hard for the reader to follow the story.

Think about a time when you went to an exciting place. List several exciting parts of your trip.

_____

_____

_____

_____

_____

_____

Write a focused story about your trip. To help focus your writing, think about a specific moment on your trip that was especially great. Use another sheet of paper if needed.

_____

_____

_____

_____

_____

_____

Mini-Lesson

Creating a Title

A title has great influence on the reader. An interesting title can increase the reader's curiosity, while a boring title might reduce the reader's interest. Students will learn to create titles that are both interesting and relevant.

Mini-Lesson:

- Ask students what makes them select a book at a library or bookstore. Is it the content? The illustrations? The title?

- Explain to students that the title is often the first clue the reader gets about a story. An appealing title will interest the reader. A boring title will give the impression that the story is also boring.

- Write the titles on the board:

  <u>Peter's Life</u>

  <u>Tales of a Fourth Grade Nothing</u>

- Ask students which title is more appealing. Discuss why *Tales of a Fourth Grade Nothing* is a more interesting title.

- Explain that a title should be appropriate and fit the story. Then, give students suggestions for writing interesting titles:

  1. A title can be a character's name. *(Matilda)*
  2. A title can name a place. *(Old Penn Station)*
  3. A title can have a hidden meaning that is revealed in the story. *(Freckle Juice)*
  4. A title can be an event or an action. *(Grandfather's Journey)*

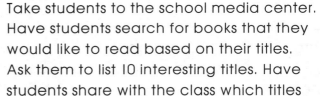

Extension

Take students to the school media center. Have students search for books that they would like to read based on their titles. Ask them to list 10 interesting titles. Have students share with the class which titles they found interesting and why.

Book List

Examples of attention-grabbing titles include *Because of Winn-Dixie, Diary of a Wimpy Kid, James and the Giant Peach, Miss Nelson Is Missing,* and *There's a Boy in the Girls' Bathroom.*

Creating a Title

Creating an interesting **title** for your writing will make readers want to read more. If a title is boring, the reader may think that the story will also be boring.

Read the pairs of titles. Write *yes* beside the title in each pair that is more interesting. The first one has been done for you.

1. A. _____ <u>Dogs</u>

   B. __*yes*__ <u>The Day I Adopted My Dog</u>

2. A. _____ <u>My Baby Sister</u>

   B. _____ <u>Stinky Diapers</u>

3. A. _____ <u>My Trip to Colorado</u>

   B. _____ <u>Sledding on the Mountain</u>

4. A. _____ <u>Cinderella Goes to a Party</u>

   B. _____ <u>Dress-Up Day</u>

5. A. _____ <u>My Best Friend</u>

   B. _____ <u>Movie Day with Jenny</u>

6. A. _____ <u>Yum . . . Pasta Salad!</u>

   B. _____ <u>My Favorite Foods</u>

7. A. _____ <u>The Best Present</u>

   B. _____ <u>A Guitar for Sam</u>

8. A. _____ <u>Fun in the Sun</u>

   B. _____ <u>Summer Is My Favorite Season</u>

Name _____   Date _____

Creating a Title

Creating an interesting **title** for your writing will make readers want to read more. If a title is boring, the reader may think that the story will also be boring.

Read the titles. Imagine that you will write about these topics. Rewrite the titles so that they are interesting and focus on your topic.

Example: My Hobbies

Stamps from Around the World

1. How I Spent My Weekend

_____

2. My Neighbor

_____

3. My Friends

_____

4. The Surprise Party

_____

5. Going to the Mall

_____

6. My Hamster

_____

7. My Favorite TV Show

_____

8. April Fools' Day

_____

Creating a Title

Creating an interesting **title** for your writing will make readers want to read more. If a title is boring, the reader may think that the story will also be boring.

Read the prompts. Imagine that you will write a story for each one. Use each strategy to write an interesting title for your story. For each story, circle the title that you think is the most interesting.

1. You have been selected to go on a space mission. Your story will tell what happens on your trip into space. Write three titles for your story.

Hidden Meaning	Place	Event or Action

2. You have been asked to take care of a neighbor's pet for two days. Your story will tell what happens while the pet is in your home. Write three titles for your story.

Hidden Meaning	Place	Event or Action

3. You were carrying your science project to class when you tripped. Your story will describe what happened to your project and what you did next. Write three titles for your story.

Hidden Meaning	Place	Event or Action

Mini-Lesson

Creating a Character

Characterization is an important element of writing fiction. Authors can strengthen their narratives by creating believable, interesting characters.

Mini-Lesson:

- Tell each student to close her eyes and visualize a good friend. Ask students to think about how their friends behave, think, speak, and feel.

- Ask students to share some characteristics that describe their friends. List the characteristics on the board.

- Explain to students that characters in fictional stories and movies have specific character traits. We learn about their personalities from the ways they act, speak, and think, as well as through their physical descriptions.

- Write the example on the board:

> The line at the movie theater seemed longer than ever. Pedro rapidly tapped his foot against the tile floor. He counted the people in front of him in line several times and rolled his eyes. "Can't these people hurry up?" he asked his mother as he let out a heavy sigh.

- Ask students what they can tell about Pedro's personality from reading the paragraph. Guide them into understanding that he may be impatient or anxious.

- Ask students to tell you how an eager student might behave in class and what a shy student may be thinking. Write their responses on the board.

- Tell students that creating authentic characters will enhance their writing.

- If necessary, reinforce this concept by creating additional examples with these character traits:

Character Traits		
bossy	confident	courageous
frustrated	gentle	graceful
grouchy	lively	strict

Name _____ Date _____

Creating a Character

Creating believable **characters** brings life to an author's writing. The way a character thinks, speaks, and behaves helps the reader understand the character's actions.

Many authors create characters based on people they know in real life. Think about someone who is special to you: a parent, a brother or sister, a friend, etc. Draw the character's face in the middle of this page. Then, answer the questions.

What does the
character look like?

1. _____

2. _____

3. _____

What does the
character think?

1. _____

2. _____

3. _____

How does the
character act?

1. _____

2. _____

3. _____

What does the
character feel?

1. _____

2. _____

3. _____

Character's Name

_____

Name _____ Date _____

Creating a Character

Creating believable **characters** brings life to an author's writing. The way a character thinks, speaks, and behaves helps the reader understand the character's actions.

Read each example. Choose a trait from the word bank that best describes the character. Write the word on the line. Then, underline the word clues that helped you figure out your answer.

Character Traits Word Bank		
charming	considerate	encouraging
excited	intelligent	strict

1. The teacher walked to the front of the room. "There will be no talking in class,"she stated firmly. "And, we will have one hour of homework each night, even on Fridays." The look in her eyes told students that she was serious.

   The teacher is _____ .

2. "Saturday mornings are the best!" announced John as he jumped out of bed. "I love sleeping late." John continued to smile while he put on his favorite T-shirt. "I can't wait to hang out with my friends!"

   John is _____ .

3. Anna earns an A on each reading assignment. She reads every night before she goes to bed. On Saturdays, her mother takes her to the library so that she has plenty to read during the week. Last year, Anna was the spelling bee champion. She believes that her love of reading has made her a great student.

   Anna is _____ .

 Extra: Create a character based on a trait in the word bank. On another sheet of paper, write a paragraph describing how your character acts.

Name _____ Date _____

Creating a Character

Creating believable **characters** brings life to an author's writing. The way a character thinks, speaks, and behaves helps the reader understand the character's actions.

Read the examples. Write an example of how each character would respond.

1. During a math lesson in school, how would a lazy student behave? _____

_____

_____

How would an eager student behave? _____

_____

_____

How would a confused student behave? _____

_____

_____

2. During dinner, what would a polite child say? _____

_____

_____

What would a hungry child say? _____

_____

_____

What would a picky child say? _____

_____

_____

 Extra: Choose one character whose response you described. On another sheet of paper, write a story about this character. Let your character's personality guide your writing.

Mini-Lesson

Describing the Setting

The settings that authors choose can play an integral part in their stories. Students will learn how the setting can influence the plots and characters of their stories.

Mini-Lesson:

- Ask students what they like to do during spring break. Then, ask them how their spring activities would be different if they lived in a different climate. For example, if they live in a warm climate, ask them to imagine that they live in Alaska.

- Tell students that their setting determines many of their activities. Explain that settings can determine what happens in stories as well.

- Tell students to imagine that they will write a story about a day at school. Ask them to describe their classroom setting. Tell them to use the five senses to help them get started. Write their descriptions on the board.

- Explain to students that a setting includes not only place but also time (past, present, time of year) and the environment (weather, scenery).

- If students need additional practice, have them use their five senses to describe other settings, such as a garage, a barn, and a grocery store.

> The smell of sweaty bodies and even sweatier socks fills the classroom. Metal chair legs screech as we flop to our seats. The air is so hot and thick that you can almost taste it. My PE class has finally finished the spring mile run!

Book List

Share examples of stories in which the setting is integral to the story. Stories include *Cloudy With a Chance of Meatballs*; *Pink and Say*; *The Relatives Came*; and *Sarah, Plain and Tall*.

Describing the Setting

Authors describe the **setting** of a story to help create the plot. When describing the setting, they think about the place, time, and surroundings of the story.

Use the five senses to describe each setting. Do not use all of the senses for each example. Include vivid details in your description.

1. The attic of a house in the winter: _____

_____

_____

2. A lighthouse near the ocean: _____

_____

_____

3. A flower garden in a park: _____

_____

_____

4. A storage shed during a thunderstorm: _____

_____

_____

5. A crowded elevator: _____

_____

_____

Describing the Setting

Authors describe the **setting** of a story to help create the plot. When describing the setting, they think about the place, time, and surroundings of the story.

The setting of a fairy tale is important to its plot. Read each situation. Describe how the change in setting would have affected the story.

1. What if a rainstorm had prevented the Big Bad Wolf from reaching the third little pig's house?

_____

_____

_____

_____

2. What if *Cinderella* had taken place today instead of once upon a time?

_____

_____

_____

_____

3. What if the three bears had lived in an apartment in the city instead of in a cottage in the woods?

_____

_____

_____

_____

Describing the Setting

Authors describe the **setting** of a story to help create the plot. When describing the setting, they think about the place, time, and surroundings of the story.

1. Write a paragraph describing your bedroom and the things that you enjoy doing there. Use the five senses to help you write your description.

_____

_____

_____

_____

_____

_____

_____

2. Imagine that you live in a castle on top of a hill. Write a paragraph describing your bedroom in the castle and the things that you would enjoy doing there. Use the five senses to help you write your description.

_____

_____

_____

_____

_____

_____

_____

Mini-Lesson

Elaboration: Show, Don't Tell

Elaboration is the use of vivid details and clear descriptions to enhance writing. It is important to teach the difference between a telling sentence and a showing sentence so that students understand the importance of elaboration.

Telling Sentences	Showing Sentences
Grandma was happy.	Ms. Smith walked over to Johnny with a wide, bright smile on her face. "Congratulations! You passed your math test!" she cheered. She high-fived Johnny and patted him on the back.
The baby is cute.	Dion had rosy cheeks and skin as soft as velvet. His lips were shaped like a little bow. He made sweet goo-goo noises, and his clothes were the size of a doll's.

Mini-Lesson:

- Explain that good authors use details to describe characters, settings, and events. This skill is called elaboration. When an author elaborates, he uses showing sentences instead of telling sentences.

- Write the sentence on the board: The dog is smart.

- Explain that this is an example of a telling sentence.

- Ask students to think about a smart dog. What does she look like? What does she do? Write sentences that show how the dog is smart.

Telling Sentences:

It was a nice day.	The house was old.
The party was fun.	My room was a mess.
The apple tasted good.	The flower was beautiful.
The movie was good.	The puppy was cute.

- Write the telling sentences from the chart on sentence strips. Divide the class into small groups. Give each group of students a sentence strip with a telling sentence. Ask each group to write several showing sentences to replace the telling sentence. Share and discuss.

Book List

Books with examples of elaboration/showing sentences include: *Brave Irene; Come On, Rain; James and the Giant Peach; Miss Nelson Is Missing; Night in the Country; The Polar Express;* and *Tales of a Fourth Grade Nothing.*

Show, Don't Tell

Good authors elaborate. Elaboration means that you "show, don't tell." A **showing sentence** has a lot of details that help the reader picture what you are writing about. A **telling sentence** makes a statement and does not include details.

Read each pair of descriptions. Decide which description is telling and which is showing. Write *T* for telling and *S* for showing.

1. A. _____   The house was old.

    B. _____   Dust sat on every piece of furniture. Two front steps were missing, and the front door hung off its hinges. Some of the windows were broken, and paint was peeling from the walls.

2. A. _____   The cheese melted in her mouth, and the tomato sauce bubbled on her tongue.

    B. _____   The pizza was delicious.

3. A. _____   Eating healthy food is important for your body.

    B. _____   The calcium in milk and yogurt helps make your bones strong. The protein in cheese and chicken helps keep your body healthy.

4. A. _____   The bracelet was very special to me.

    B. _____   My great-grandmother gave me a bracelet when I was born. It belonged to her. I wear it only on special occasions, and it makes me think of her.

5. A. _____   I ran to the door, threw it open, and yelled, "Get in here this minute!"

    B. _____   I was furious.

6. A. _____   Socks were scattered on the floor. Comic books and magazines peeked out from under the bed. The bedspread lay on the floor in a heap.

    B. _____   My room was a disaster!

Show, Don't Tell

Good authors elaborate. Elaboration means using **showing sentences** with many details to help the reader picture what you are writing about. A **telling sentence** makes a statement and does not include details.

What is the author *showing* in these sentences? Write the *telling* sentences. The first one has been done for you.

1. Showing: My heart beat loudly in my chest, and my hands trembled. I felt the sweat pouring down my forehead, and I wondered, "Will I really be able to do this?"

   Telling: I was <u>nervous</u>.

2. Showing: The fruit salad was a colorful mix of pineapple, grapes, oranges, and apples covered in chopped nuts. My mouth watered as I grabbed the spoon.

   Telling: The fruit salad was _____ .

3. Showing: My father burst into my room, waving my report card in the air. He cheered, "You did it! You did it!" Then, he ran to me and gave me a big hug.

   Telling: My father was _____ .

These are *telling* sentences. Change them into *showing* sentences.

4. Telling: I was very angry.

   Showing: I was as furious as a _____ .

   I said, " _____ ."

   Then, _____

   _____ .

5. Telling: I was very excited.

   Showing: I was so thrilled that I felt like a _____ .

   I _____ and

   _____ .

   I said, " _____ ."

Show, Don't Tell

Good authors elaborate. Elaboration means using showing sentences instead of telling sentences. A **showing sentence** includes details and a description to help the reader picture what you are writing about. A **telling sentence** makes a statement and does not include details. Using the five senses will help you elaborate when you write.

Change the *telling sentences* into *showing sentences* by adding details. Use your five senses to help you fill in the blanks.

1. Telling sentence: It was the best cake I've ever had!

   The cake looked _____ .

   The cake smelled _____ .

   In my mouth, the cake felt _____ .

   The cake tasted _____ .

   Use your descriptions to write a few showing sentences about the cake.

   _____

   _____

   _____

2. Telling sentence: It was a great party.

   What did you see at the party?_____

   What did you hear at the party? _____

   What did you eat at the party? _____

   How did the things you listed look, sound, or taste? Describe the party using a few showing sentences.

   _____

   _____

   _____

Mini-Lesson

Creating Dialogue

Dialogue between characters is a powerful way to improve writing. Dialogue makes a story more interesting and authentic, helps the story flow for the reader, and brings the characters to life.

Mini-Lesson:

Write these tips on the board.

Tip #1: Dialogue should be sprinkled throughout a story. It should not be the entire story. Other words must be used within the story to explain what is happening while the characters are talking. Otherwise, it can be confusing for the reader.

> Shy Character: "I . . . I don't know the answer to that one," Annie mumbled timidly.
>
> Villain: "I will rule this kingdom. No one can stop me!" he yelled with an angry voice.

Tip #2: The personality of a character and his situation should determine how dialogue is written. It is important to keep dialogue true to characters and events.

> Example: "What was that?" asked Tom.
>
> Better: "What was that?" Tom whispered nervously as a loud crash echoed through the hallway.

Tip #3: Expand dialogue with specific action and dialogue tags. A dialogue tag tells who is talking and how the words are being spoken.

Extension

Cut out pictures of people in action from magazines and catalogs. Have students imagine what the characters are saying and write dialogue for the characters.

Name _____   Date _____

Creating Dialogue

A **dialogue tag** tells who is talking and how the words are being spoken.

Examples of dialogue tags:

José said   answered Carina   Walter replied   mumbled Melanie

Complete the dialogue tags using words from the word bank. Choose a word that best fits what the character is saying or doing. Words may be used more than once.

Dialogue Tags Word Bank

admitted	begged	cheered	confessed
explained	giggled	warned	whispered

1. "Can we please stay for 10 more minutes?" _____ the children.

2. "I knew about the surprise party all along!" Jonah _____ .

3. "That was a really silly joke," Alyssa _____ .

4. "I'm catching a cold. Don't get too close," _____ Maggie.

5. "Shh, she might hear us," _____ Liz.

6. "I didn't mean to do it," Serena _____ .

7. "You can do it!" _____ the cheerleaders.

8. "First, line up all of the numbers. Then, add them," _____ the teacher.

9. "The water in the pool is chilly today," _____ the lifeguard.

10. "Stir the ingredients well," _____ the cooking instructor.

Creating Dialogue

Authors can make **dialogue** stronger by expanding sentences to show what characters are doing or what is happening while they are talking.

Draw a line from each sentence beginning to the phrase that expands it.

1. "I'm ready for school, Mom," said Scott
2. "Let me see the trophy!" shouted Ms. Soler
3. "I think I need a bath," giggled Abigail

A. after the class won the competition.
B. after falling in the mud pit during the tug-of-war.
C. just as he finished tying his shoes.

Expand each sentence by showing what the characters are doing as they talk.

4. "Do you think that it will rain?" asked Alfonso as _____

_____ .

5. "Take your seats right away," hurried Ms. Lora when _____

_____ .

6. "I am so proud of you," smiled my dad after _____

_____ .

7. "Let's get ready for the party," announced my mother while _____

_____ .

8. "I'll beat you to the finish line!" squealed Tabatha as _____

_____ .

9. "Sure, I'll do it," answered Heather, although _____

_____ .

10. "He might do it this time!" shrieked Joey while _____

_____ .

Creating Dialogue

Authors can make **dialogue** stronger by expanding sentences to show what characters are doing or what is happening while they are talking.

Read each sentence beginning. Choose a word from the word bank and write an expanded phrase for each sentence.

Word Bank				
after	although	as	because	before
in	since	when	while	with

Examples:

"I'm ready for school, Mom," shouted Scott, *although* he still had on his pajamas.

"I've had enough!" moaned Jermaine *after* doing 100 jumping jacks.

1. "I never thought that would happen," mumbled Chandra _____

_____ .

2. "We need to go right away," urged Sammy _____

_____ .

3. "What did you get me?" asked Opal _____

_____ .

Write expanded dialogue for each character. Remember that the dialogue should sound like something that the character would say. Imagine that the characters are on a field trip to the zoo. What might each character say? How would he say it? What might he be doing while he says it?

4. A shy student: _____

_____ .

5. The teacher: _____

_____ .

6. A student who wants to be a zookeeper when she grows up: _____

_____ .

Mini-Lesson

Writing for Your Audience

A good author knows her audience. Identifying the audience helps the author determine the format, content, and word choice of written pieces.

Mini-Lesson:

- Ask students how they greet their friends at school. Then, ask them how they greet their teachers.

- Tell students that what people say and how they say it depends on whom they say it to. The same concept applies to writing. When we write, our audience helps determine what we write and how we write it.

- Ask students to imagine that they each received a scooter as a gift from a friend. Tell them that they each will write two thank-you notes—one to the friend and one to the friend's parents. Remind students to let the audience guide the content and word choice of their notes.

- Use the sample notes or have students help you write two new thank-you notes.

Dear Byron,

Thank you for the new scooter. It's so cool! It's just like the scooter we saw at the park last summer. I can't wait until the weather warms up and we can go to the park again. It's going to be awesome! All the kids will want to ride my scooter. Maybe I can get my mom to buy one for you too. That would be a blast!

Thanks again,

Joey

Dear Mr. and Mrs. Quinn,

I would like to thank you for the fantastic gift. I have always wanted a scooter! I am sure that I will have a wonderful time riding it in the park. My family and I appreciate your thoughtfulness.

Sincerely,

Joe Brady

Writing for Your Audience

Authors think about their **audience** when deciding what to write about and how to write it. Knowing their audience guides the way that they write.

Read each paragraph. Decide who the audience is. Choose an answer from the word bank and write it on the line.

Audience Word Bank			
family member	friend	government office	teacher

1. I am a fourth grader at Maple Grove Elementary School. We are learning about recycling in our community. I thought that it would be an excellent idea to start a recycling program at our school. Think of all of the paper that teachers and students throw away each day! Would you please tell me what steps I need to follow to begin a recycling program at my school?

_____

2. Thank you for taking us to the playground this weekend. My brother and I don't get to see our cousins very often, so it was great to spend so much time just playing together. I hope that we can do it again soon!

_____

3. I had an awesome time on my school field trip. It was so much fun! The zookeeper let us watch the lions eat. I think that we should try to get our dads to take us to the zoo together. That would be so cool!

_____

4. I learned many interesting things about giraffes while researching animals for my report. First, I learned that a giraffe's tongue measures up to 18 inches (45 cm). I found out that giraffes are some of the most peaceful animals on Earth. I also discovered that giraffes can survive long periods of time without water.

_____

 Extra: Circle the key words in each passage that helped you select your answer.

Name _____   Date _____

Writing for Your Audience

Authors think about their **audience** when deciding what to write about and how to write it. Knowing their audience guides the way that they write.

Imagine that you are running for class president. Plan a speech telling your classmates why they should vote for you. Answer the questions to help you plan the content of your speech.

1. Who is my audience? _____

_____

2. What is important to my audience? _____

_____

_____

3. What is my audience least likely to care about? _____

_____

_____

4. What do I want my audience to know about me? _____

_____

_____

5. What is the best way to organize my writing for my audience? ____

_____

_____

_____

 Extra: Think about how your answers would change if your speech were written for your teacher instead of for your classmates.

Writing for Your Audience

Authors think about their **audience** when deciding what to write about and how to write it. Knowing their audience guides the way that they write.

Imagine that you forgot to bring a pencil to school. Write two notes asking to borrow a pencil. Write one note to a classmate you know well. Write the other note to your teacher.

Note to a Classmate

_____

_____

_____

_____

_____

_____

_____

Note to Your Teacher

_____

_____

_____

_____

_____

_____

_____

Mini-Lesson

Voice

Voice is an abstract concept for some students. It shows the author's personality and style. Reproduce the samples and display them in the classroom to demonstrate the use of voice in student writing.

Writing Without Voice:

My best friend, Amanda, is great. She is always there for me when I need her. I am very thankful that she is my friend.

Writing with Voice:

My friend, Amanda, is the very best friend that I could ever have. She is always there for me, no matter what. All I have to do is ask. She helps me study for tests, gives me advice, and cheers me up with silly jokes! When people ask me about Amanda, I always say, "Yep! That's my best friend!" I am super lucky to have her in my life!

Mini-Lesson:

- After reviewing the writing samples, explain to students that they should "write like they talk" and their writing should "sound like them."

- Explain to students that you will show them the importance of voice through storytelling. Tell students that you will tell them two versions of a story about a trip that you took. Their job is to decide which version of your story "sounds more like you." Share a story with versions similar to those below.

Version #1: This weekend, I went to the beach. It was a beautiful, sunny day. I took my favorite book and read. I ate lunch under my umbrella too. It was a great day.

Version #2: I went to the beach this weekend and spent the whole day there. It was beautiful! I mean, it was a perfect sunny day—the kind you just want to spend outside. I had been dying to go to the beach, because it had been a long week and I just needed to relax and enjoy myself. I planted my umbrella in the sand, took out my favorite book, nibbled on my sandwich, and read in the shade. It was exactly what I needed!

, • Ask students to discuss which version sounded more authentic and more like you. Explain that this is an example of voice, and it applies to writing as well as speaking.

• Have students practice using voice by role-playing with partners. Each student should select a topic and tell a story about it. (It helps if students are excited about their topics so that their storytelling is not forced.) After partners have completed the exercise twice, have them practice applying this skill by writing some of their sentences and stories. Discuss how words, phrases, and sentences can affect the voice of the writing as well as reveal the author's personality and mood.

Tips:

• Record each student talking about a topic or storytelling. Then, play the story back so that each student can hear her voice before she writes.

• When a student experiences writer's block, have him talk about his topic with a partner. By doing so, a student can often find his voice and get new ideas about what should be included in his writing.

Book List

Books with great examples of voice include *Because of Winn-Dixie*, *Dear Mr. Henshaw*, and *James and the Giant Peach*.

Voice

Good writing has voice. That means that an author's writing should sound like him or her. Voice makes an author's writing more interesting.

Read the examples.

No voice: I went with my best friend to the amusement park. We rode the Ferris wheel. It was high. I screamed a lot. My friend thought that it was funny.

Voice: My best friend and I went to the amusement park. The first thing that we rode was the Ferris wheel. Trust me when I say that it was a bad idea! The Ferris wheel is super high, and I screamed from the moment we got on until we got off. I never stopped! Can you believe that all my friend did was laugh?

Read each pair of writing samples. Write *yes* if the writing has voice. Write *no* if the writing does not have voice.

1. A. _____ Boy, did Bobby get in trouble in class today! Do you want to know what he did? He took the shavings from the pencil sharpener and dumped them on his desk to see what was in there. What a mess! Our teacher almost exploded!

   B. _____ Bobby got in trouble in school today. He emptied the pencil sharpener on his desk. Our teacher was really mad.

2. A. _____ I think that we should have school only four days a week. Then, we could have Fridays off and have more time to do fun things. If I were in charge, that would be my rule.

   B. _____ If I were in charge, guess what I would do? I would cancel school on Fridays! Then, we would have to go to school only four days a week and we'd have more time to do things like sleep, play outside, watch television, and hang out with our friends. That would be so cool!

3. A. _____ This was the time to do it! I had to be brave. I needed to show that I could! I took a deep breath and stepped onto the stage for my big performance.

   B. _____ I was really nervous about going on stage for my performance.

Voice

Good writing has voice. That means that an author's writing should sound like him or her. Voice makes an author's writing more interesting.

Read the examples.

No voice: I went with my best friend to the amusement park. We rode the Ferris wheel. It was high. I screamed a lot. My friend thought that it was funny.

Voice: My best friend and I went to the amusement park. The first thing that we rode was the Ferris wheel. Trust me when I say that it was a bad idea! The Ferris wheel is super high, and I screamed from the moment we got on until we got off. I never stopped! Can you believe that all my friend did was laugh?

This story includes good examples of voice. Read the story. Underline the words, phrases, and sentences that are good examples of voice.

Sometimes, I wish that my little brother would stop following me around. I know that sounds mean, but it's true! If you had a little brother like Erik, you would feel the same way. Trust me. This morning I was dressed and ready to go to school. Just as I was about to grab my things and catch the bus, who drops an entire bowl of wet, soggy, mushy, disgusting cereal on my backpack? Erik, of course. He is like a two-year-old tornado!

Extra: Reread one of your writing assignments. Does it sound like you? Does your personality shine through? On another sheet of paper, rewrite any sections that need more voice.

Voice

Good writing has voice. That means that an author's writing should sound like him or her. Voice makes an author's writing more interesting.

Read the examples:

No voice: I went with my best friend to the amusement park. We rode the Ferris wheel. It was high. I screamed a lot. My friend thought that it was funny.

Voice: My best friend and I went to the amusement park. The first thing that we rode was the Ferris wheel. Trust me when I say that it was a bad idea! The Ferris wheel is super high, and I screamed from the moment we got on until we got off. I never stopped! Can you believe that all my friend did was laugh?

Rewrite each example so that it has voice and sounds more interesting.

1. **No voice:** The teacher was really proud. Everyone in the class had passed the test.

   Voice: _____

   _____

   _____

2. **No voice:** My friend and I wanted to sing in the school talent show. I was worried that I would not do a good job. A lot of kids signed up. I was nervous, but I really wanted to sing with my friend. So, I wrote my name beside hers on the sign-up sheet.

   Voice: _____

   _____

   _____

 Extra: Underline the words in the paragraph that make the story interesting and give it voice.

   My heart boomed as I buckled my seat belt. I had waited to ride the Super Loop for weeks! As the roller coaster took off, I knew that the wait had been worth it. "Yippee!" I yelled as it zoomed through the air. It went so fast that when it was over, I double-checked to see if my head was still there. I was sure that it had flown off on the big loop!

Point of View

Mini-Lesson

Point of view refers to the perspective from which a story is told. This lesson will help students think critically about the characters that they create and how different characters should interpret situations differently.

Mini-Lesson:

- Begin by sharing the story *Julius, the Baby of the World* by Kevin Henkes. Tell students that the story is about a girl named Lilly and her little brother, Julius. The story is told from Lilly's point of view.

- Explain that point of view refers to how a character views the world or a situation.

- After reading the story, ask students to describe Lilly—her personality, her behavior, and her feelings. List these characteristics on the board.

- Then, ask students to describe Julius. What might he be feeling? What might he be thinking? List the ideas on the board.

- Tell students to focus on Julius. What if *he* had told the story? How would it be different? List possible scenarios on the board.

- Have students rewrite the story from Julius's point of view.

- Ask students to share their stories.

Book List
You can substitute the story used in this lesson with any story that includes characters with different points of view. Examples include: *The Great Kapok Tree*, *Lilly's Purple Plastic Purse*, *The Pain and the Great One*, and *Where the Wild Things Are*.

Point of View

Point of view refers to how people or characters view objects and situations. Different characters can look at the same situation in different ways.

Read each statement. Tell how each person or object might feel in each situation.

1. A family is sitting down to have a picnic in the park.

   A. How might the family feel? _____

   _____

   B. How might a nearby ant feel? _____

   _____

2. A boy is playing fetch with his dog.

   A. How might the boy feel? _____

   _____

   B. How might the dog feel? _____

   _____

3. A teacher is preparing to give a test to her students.

   A. How might the teacher feel? _____

   _____

   B. How might her students feel? _____

   _____

4. A child is getting ready to ice-skate for the first time.

   A. How might the child feel? _____

   _____

   B. How might the child's parents feel? _____

   _____

Point of View

Point of view refers to how people or characters view objects and situations. Different characters can look at the same situation in different ways.

Read the story and follow the directions.

Rosa is turning nine today. She thought that she would be celebrating her special day with her family. When she wakes up, it seems that no one has remembered her birthday. Rosa does not know that the whole family has a big surprise party planned for that evening, complete with cake, presents, and all of her friends!

1. Describe how Rosa might feel. _____

_____

_____

2. What are some things that Rosa might say? _____

_____

_____

3. Describe how the family might feel. _____

_____

_____

4. What are some things that her family members might say? _____

_____

_____

_____

Name _____   Date _____

Point of View

Point of view refers to how people or characters view objects and situations. Different characters can look at the same situation in different ways.

Read the story. Think about how each person or object would view the situation. Write a paragraph for each point of view. Write it as if the person or object were telling the story.

Mr. Fernandez is a fifth-grade teacher. Today, he came to school wearing one black shoe and one brown shoe! He did not realize what he was wearing until he arrived at school. During recess, he went home to change his shoes.

1. Mr. Fernandez's point of view:

_____

_____

_____

_____

2. The point of view of a student who is not in Mr. Fernandez's class: _____

_____

_____

_____

_____

3. The point of view of the black and the brown shoes: _____

_____

_____

_____

_____

Vivid Vocabulary

Mini-Lesson

Authors use adjectives to help the reader see, hear, taste, smell, or feel what they are describing. Selecting specific, accurate words will help students clearly express their intended meanings.

Mini-Lesson:

- Write the sentences on the board:

  My parents will be <u>happy</u> if I get an A on my test.

  My parents will be <u>happy</u> if I do all of my chores for a month.

  My parents will be <u>happy</u> if I win the science fair.

- Ask students how their parents would feel in each situation. Write some responses on the board.

- Explain that the word *happy* is not strong enough to describe how parents would really feel. Tell students that selecting strong words to describe feelings in their writing will help them communicate more effectively.

- Create a list of synonyms for *happy* on the board. (See the chart below.) Have students replace *happy* in each sentence above with a more exact word. For example:

  My parents will be <u>overjoyed</u> if I win the science fair.

- Follow the same procedure for this sentence:

  I was <u>mad</u> when my swim team lost the race.

- Display the lists of synonyms in the classroom.

Happy		Mad	
content	delighted	angry	annoyed
joyful	merry	fuming	furious
pleased	thrilled	heated	upset

Vivid Vocabulary

It is important for authors to select the best words, or **vivid vocabulary**, to describe feelings in their writing.

Example: Julia was <u>happy</u> when her uncle returned after being away for two years.

Better: Julia was <u>overjoyed</u> when her uncle returned after being away for two years.

Happy is not strong enough to express how Julia felt in this situation. *Overjoyed* describes her feelings better.

Fill in the word bank. If necessary, use a thesaurus to write a list of at least five synonyms for each word. Refer to this list when you are looking for just the right word to use in your writing.

Feelings Word Bank		
Words That Mean **Good**	Words That Mean **Bad**	Words That Mean **Nice**
Words That Mean **Sad**	Words That Mean **Scared**	Words That Mean **Tired**

Vivid Vocabulary

It is important for authors to select **vivid vocabulary** to describe feelings in their writing.

Example: Julia was <u>happy</u> when her uncle returned after being away for two years.

Better: Julia was <u>overjoyed</u> when her uncle returned after being away for two years.

Happy is not strong enough to express how Julia felt in this situation. *Overjoyed* describes her feelings better.

Rewrite each sentence so that it includes vivid vocabulary. Replace the underlined word with a word that more clearly describes the feeling.

1. I was <u>glad</u> to learn that I would soon have a baby brother. _____

_____

2. My sister wants a pet snake, but I am <u>scared</u> of snakes. _____

_____

3. My cousin is <u>nice</u>. She offered to help me study. _____

_____

4. Iesha had a <u>good</u> time in dance class. _____

_____

5. I was so <u>mad</u> when I dropped my ice-cream cone. _____

_____

6. I am too <u>scared</u> to watch the new thriller movie! _____

_____

7. Mrs. Lee was <u>happy</u> when all of her students passed the test. _____

_____

8. I was <u>sad</u> when my painting was not chosen for the art contest. _____

_____

Name _____ Date _____

Vivid Vocabulary

It is important for authors to select **vivid vocabulary** to describe feelings in their writing.

Example: Julia was <u>happy</u> when her uncle returned after being away for two years.

Better: Julia was <u>overjoyed</u> when her uncle returned after being away for two years.

Happy is not strong enough to express how Julia felt in this situation. *Overjoyed* describes her feelings better.

Read the example. Then, write sentences accurately describing your emotions.

Example: You scraped your knee while playing soccer.
         I was annoyed that I scraped my knee during my soccer game.

1. You just received the gift that you were hoping for. _____

_____

2. Your mom let you have an extra helping of your favorite meal at dinner. _____

_____

3. You made a new friend. _____

_____

4. You watched a mysterious movie scene. _____

_____

5. You lost your lunch money. _____

_____

6. You are going to the dentist. _____

_____

7. You are going shopping for school supplies. _____

_____

   Step Up to Writing · CD-104384 · © Carson-Dellosa

Using Stronger Verbs

Mini-Lesson

Action verbs add motion and interest to an author's writing. Strong verbs describe specific action and give more detail.

Tired, passive, or helping verbs = boring sentences	Stronger, more-specific verbs = better sentences
The race car <u>goes really fast</u>.	The race car <u>zooms</u>.
Katrina <u>came</u> into the classroom.	Katrina <u>dashed</u> into the classroom.
The boys <u>went</u> into the pool.	The boys <u>dove</u> into the pool.

Mini-Lesson:

- If necessary, review adjectives, nouns, verbs, and adverbs. Explain that although these are parts of speech, they are also authors' tools. Verbs make characters and actions come alive.

- Write this sentence on the board: *I heard the tires make a noise as the car came around the corner.*

- Ask students to describe the noise the car might make. List active, specific verbs to describe the noise (screech, roar, thunder, squeal). Rewrite the sentence with a stronger verb. Next, ask how the car might have come around the corner. Did it swerve? Did it speed? Did it skid? Rewrite the sentence with stronger verbs: *I heard the car screech as it swerved around the corner.* Discuss which sentence is better and why.

Follow the same procedure for these sentences:

Example 1: *Juan went to the store.*

Better: *Juan biked to the store.*

Example 2: *I walked all around the garden and looked at the butterflies.*

Better: *I tiptoed around the garden and admired the butterflies.*

Example 3: *Lightning appeared in the sky.*

Better: *The lightning flashed and crackled.*

Using Stronger Verbs

Verbs add action to an author's writing. Good authors use strong, exact verbs.

Circle the verbs or verb phrases that make each sentence stronger and more specific.

1. When Casey heard the doorbell, he (went, flew) to the door.

2. My mother (scolded, said), "Shhh! You will wake the baby!"

3. The thunder (scared, terrified) me.

4. "I can't catch my breath!" (wheezed, said) Tommy.

5. Amanda (skipped, went) to the store for apples and bread.

6. The flag (moved, danced) in the heavy winds.

7. We all (went on, rode) the roller coaster.

8. Brian nervously (performed, did) his juggling act in front of the whole class.

9. The energetic dog (ran, chased) after the tennis ball.

10. Emily (sat, relaxed) on the couch.

Name _____   Date _____

Using Stronger Verbs

Verbs add action to an author's writing. Good authors use strong, exact verbs.

Replace the underlined verbs and verb phrases with more specific, stronger verbs from the word bank.

Verbs Word Bank			
explored	floated	flopped	gasped
grumbled	peeked	poured	scribbled

1. "You would not believe what I just saw!" <u>said</u> Beth.

   "You would not believe what I just saw!" _____ Beth.

2. Brenda <u>came</u> down the stairs, looking like a princess in her beautiful dress.

   Brenda _____ down the stairs, looking like a princess in her beautiful dress.

3. The rain <u>came</u> into our window like a tidal wave.

   The rain _____ into our window like a tidal wave.

4. Before rushing out the door, Luke <u>wrote</u> a note to his mom.

   Before rushing out the door, Luke _____ a note to his mom.

5. Andrew <u>walked through</u> his new house.

   Andrew _____ his new house.

6. "I wish I didn't have to do the dishes today," <u>said</u> Leanne.

   "I wish I didn't have to do the dishes today," _____ Leanne.

7. I was so tired that I <u>got</u> into bed the minute I got home.

   I was so tired that I _____ into bed the minute I got home.

8. I <u>looked</u> around the brick wall.

   I _____ around the brick wall.

Using Stronger Verbs

Verbs add action to an author's writing. Good authors use strong, exact verbs.

Fill in each blank with a strong, exact, active verb.

1. She _____ home as quickly as she could.

2. The duckling _____ as she tried to keep up with her mother.

3. "Oh no!" cried the waitress as the plates _____ to the floor.

4. "I really love it when it rains," _____ Joe.

5. The baby _____ loudly while her mother prepared her bottle.

6. Maria _____ to school, eager to show her friend her new shoes.

7. The students _____ around the school, looking for their new classrooms.

8. The shy girl _____ as she began to present her report.

9. Martin's heart pounded as he _____ the starting line of the race.

10. The motorcycle _____ down the street.

Similes and Metaphors

Mini-Lesson

Making comparisons through similes and metaphors helps an author create a mental image for the reader. In this lesson, students will learn to compare objects and ideas in their writing.

Mini-Lesson:

- Write the sentence on the board:

  The man is happy.

  Ask students to visualize the happy man and describe what they see. Ask them if it is difficult to picture the man.

- Write the sentence on the board:

  The man is as happy as a kid in a candy store.

  Ask students which sentence made it easier to visualize the man and why.

- Explain that authors often describe things by comparing objects and ideas. This helps the reader create a more detailed mental image. Tell students that there are two ways to make comparisons—writing similes and writing metaphors.

- A simile compares two objects or ideas by using the words *like* or *as*. Ask students to explain the meanings of the similes.

  Examples: *Tasha's hair is as soft as silk.*

  The boy eats like a bird.

- Tell students that a metaphor compares two unlike things without using the words *like* or *as*. Ask students to explain the meanings of the metaphors.

  Examples: *My father is a pack rat.*

  When Jimmy is sleeping, he is an angel.

Book List
Ask students to search for similes and metaphors in children's books. Have students draw pictures of the images that the authors have described. Some examples include *Jumanji*, *Owl Moon*, and *Tar Beach*.

Similes and Metaphors

A **simile** compares two objects or ideas by using the words *like* or *as*.

Example: Her words were <u>as sharp as a razor</u>.

A **metaphor** compares two unlike things without using the words *like* or *as*.

Example: After the fall, my swollen ankle was <u>a red balloon</u>.

Identify whether each sentence includes a simile or a metaphor. Write *S* if the sentence includes a simile. Write *M* if the sentence includes a metaphor.

1. _____ The ocean is a hungry animal.

2. _____ Her expression was as sour as a lime.

3. _____ I dried the dishes so well that they sparkled like diamonds.

4. _____ My room is a junkyard.

5. _____ Gavin's compliment made my face turn as red as an apple.

6. _____ Bridget is a walking encyclopedia.

7. _____ The athlete was as strong as an ox.

8. _____ The student sat in class like a bump on a log.

Describe your best friend. Write one sentence using a simile and one sentence using a metaphor.

9. Simile: _____

10. Metaphor: _____

Similes and Metaphors

> A **simile** compares two objects or ideas by using the words *like* or *as*.
>
> Example: Her words were <u>as sharp as a razor</u>.
>
> A **metaphor** compares two unlike things without using the words *like* or *as*.
>
> Example: After the fall, my swollen ankle was <u>a red balloon</u>.

Complete each simile.

1. as stubborn as _____

2. as clumsy as _____

3. as loud as _____

Write a sentence using each simile that you created.

4. _____

5. _____

6. _____

Read the metaphors. Write a sentence explaining the meaning of each metaphor.

Example: He clammed up when his parents asked him who broke the vase.
        This means that he kept his mouth closed when his parents questioned him.

7. The stars were jewels in the night sky. _____

_____

8. Jessica is a treasure chest of ideas. _____

_____

9. My mind was a sponge soaking up all of her brilliant ideas. _____

_____

10. The field wore a coat of gold. _____

_____

Similes and Metaphors

A **simile** compares two objects or ideas by using the words *like* or *as*.

Example: Her words were <u>as sharp as a razor</u>.

A **metaphor** compares two unlike things without using the words *like* or *as*.

Example: After the fall, my swollen ankle was <u>a red balloon</u>.

Rewrite each sentence using a simile.

Example: Jane is busy. *Jane is as busy as a bee.*

1. The temperature felt cold. _____

_____

2. The streets are quiet in the morning. _____

_____

3. Timmy's new backpack is very light. _____

_____

4. The well near the barn is quite deep. _____

_____

Rewrite each sentence using a metaphor.

Example: I have a lot of homework to do. *I have a mountain of homework to do.*

5. The mall was crowded. _____

_____

6. The kitten is sweet. _____

_____

7. The moon is full. _____

_____

8. Henry is excited. _____

_____

Onomatopoeia

Mini-Lesson

Authors may employ onomatopoeia to enhance the reader's sensory experience with a story. Onomatopoeia is the use of a word that imitates the sound of an object.

Mini-Lesson:

- Tell students to sit still and listen. Ask them what sounds they hear. Write their responses on the board. For example, they may hear the *tick-tock* of a clock, the *hum* of an air conditioner, the *honk* from a car, or a student's *sigh*.

- Explain that these sound words are called *onomatopoeia* and that they can be used to enhance writing.

- Ask students to share other words that imitate sounds. If students are struggling, share additional examples.

- Write the sentence on the board:

  I heard the raindrops fall on the roof.

- Ask students to think of a way to add onomatopoeia to this sentence.

  Example: Plop, plop, plop. I could hear the raindrops falling on the roof.

- Pair students and have each pair create a sentence with other sounds that are associated with a rainstorm.

  Example: The swish of the wind rattled the windows.

- As students practice using onomatopoeia, be sure that they do not overuse it.

  Example: Boom! Bam! Splat! The book fell on the floor.

- Explain that onomatopoeia has a greater effect when it is not overused.

Extensions

- Many comic books use onomatopoeia. Share a few appropriate examples with students and have them identify the sound words.

- At recess, take the class outside and listen to the sounds. Create a list of onomatopoeic words based on their observations.

Name _____ Date _____

Onomatopoeia

Onomatopoeia is the use of words that copy sounds.

Select a word from the onomatopoeia word bank to complete each sentence.

Onomatopoeia Word Bank				
buzz	Ding-dong	Drip	honk	meow
roar	slurp	smack	toot	Whirr

1. The _____ of the lion vibrated through the jungle.

2. I was running in the hallway when _____! I ran right into my friend Leo.

3. _____! A hummingbird flew past my head!

4. I heard the _____ of the train as it approached the crossing.

5. The excited cat's _____ woke me up.

6. The mosquito's _____ reminded me to put on repellent.

7. _____. The faucet is leaking again!

8. I could hear the bus driver _____ her horn from my kitchen table.

9. _____ . Someone is at the door.

10. My mother always says that it is not polite to _____ your soup.

Write two sentences using onomatopoeia and underline the onomatopoeia.

11. _____

12. _____

Onomatopoeia

> **Onomatopoeia** is the use of words that copy sounds.

Different objects produce different sounds. Read the phrases. Write an onomatopoeic word for the sound that is made.

Example: A can of soda when first opened: fizz

1. A balloon bursting: _____

2. Dry leaves on branches on a breezy day: _____

3. Baby birds waiting for food in their nest: _____

4. A wolf on a mountaintop: _____

5. A door opening slowly: _____

6. Children laughing at the playground: _____

7. A rabbit hopping behind the bushes: _____

8. A hungry stomach before lunch: _____

9. A fire engine leaving the station: _____

10. Celery being eaten: _____

Imagine that you are in a crowded toy store. List six onomatopoeic words that relate to sounds heard in a toy store.

_____   _____

_____   _____

_____   _____

Onomatopoeia

Onomatopoeia is the use of words that copy sounds.

Onomatopoeia can be used to liven up your writing. Read the descriptive sentences. Rewrite each sentence so that it contains one onomatopoeic word.

Example: The race cars <u>speed</u> around the track.

Better: The race cars <u>zoom</u> around the track.

1. The wild turkeys could be heard throughout the woods. _____
_____

2. My father's keys make a sound when he opens the door. _____
_____

3. The loud motorcycle went past my house. _____
_____

4. Amanda accidentally tore her homework into two pieces. _____
_____

5. The carpenter hammered the nail into the wall. _____
_____

6. The sound of the vacuum cleaner made it difficult to hear the TV. _____
_____

7. The old door made a noise as I closed it. _____
_____

8. This cold has made me sneeze all day long! _____
_____

 Extra: Choose a previous writing assignment. Find two descriptive sentences and revise each to include onomatopoeia.

Idioms
Mini-Lesson

Some authors use idioms to add variety to their writing. An idiom is an expression with a figurative meaning that is well-known because of its common use.

Mini-Lesson:

- Ask students if they have ever heard the expression "It's raining cats and dogs."

- Ask them if it ever really rains cats and dogs. Guide them into understanding that the expression really means that it is raining heavily.

- Explain that these set phrases are called *idioms* and that the words have different meanings from what is actually written. Tell students that using idioms can add interest to their writing.

- Write the sentences on the board:

    You could <u>catch a cold</u>.

    Steve is feeling <u>under the weather</u>.

- Discuss the literal and figurative meanings of each idiom.

- Have students share idioms that they have learned from family members, friends, and characters in books and on TV. Write these expressions on the board. Discuss their literal and figurative meanings.

 ### Extension

This lesson (Idioms) and the following lesson (Personification) focus on figures of speech. Hyperbole is a third example in this category. Hyperbole uses extreme exaggeration to make a point.

Write these examples of hyperbole on the board:

I could sleep for a year.

This backpack weighs a ton!

I've heard that a million times.

Ask students to brainstorm additional examples. Write their responses on the board. Then, have students illustrate their favorite hyperboles. Invite students to guess the hyperboles illustrated by their classmates.

Idioms

An **idiom** is an expression whose true meaning is different from its literal meaning.

Example: Watching too much TV made Edward feel <u>like a couch potato</u>.

This expression means that Edward felt <u>lazy</u>, not that he felt like an actual potato on a couch.

Select your favorite idiom from the list. Write it on the line. Then, draw a picture that shows the word-by-word meaning of the idiom. Under the picture, explain what the idiom really means.

You're driving me up the wall.   I'm all ears.

She had butterflies in her stomach.   Hold your horses.

That was a piece of cake.   I'm going bananas!

Toot your own horn.   He is out to lunch.

Idioms

An **idiom** is an expression whose true meaning is different from its literal meaning.

Example: Watching too much TV made Edward feel <u>like a couch potato</u>.

This expression means that Edward felt <u>lazy</u>, not that he felt like an actual potato on a couch.

These statements contain idioms. Read the sentences. Circle the answers that give the correct meanings of the idioms.

1. Alice had butterflies in her stomach before the tennis match.

    A. was coming down with the flu

    B. was nervous

2. Tell me about it. I'm all ears.

    A. listening carefully

    B. covered in ears

3. That noise is driving me up the wall.

    A. bothering me

    B. very loud

4. Hold your horses. I am coming!

    A. stop running

    B. wait patiently

5. I'm going bananas with all of this homework!

    A. going crazy

    B. turning yellow

6. This puzzle is difficult. I'm in over my head.

    A. in deep water

    B. struggling

Idioms

An **idiom** is an expression whose true meaning is different from its literal meaning.

Example: Watching too much TV made Edward feel <u>like a couch potato</u>.

This expression means that Edward felt <u>lazy</u>, not that he felt like an actual potato on a couch.

Read the idioms. Explain what you think each one means.

1. Piece of cake: _____

2. Tongue-tied: _____

3. Over-the-hill: _____

4. Hit the sack: _____

5. All ears: _____

Write a sentence using each idiom.

6. Cat got your tongue: _____

_____

7. See eye to eye: _____

_____

8. Toot your own horn: _____

_____

 Extra: Choose a previous writing assignment. Add an idiom to the writing.

Personification

Mini-Lesson

Authors may use personification to add interest and description to their writing. Personification is a type of figurative language that gives human qualities or characteristics to something that is not human.

Mini-Lesson:

- Write the sentences on the board:

  The clouds moved across the sky on that breezy morning.

  The clouds danced across the sky on that breezy morning.

- Guide students into understanding that even though the clouds cannot really dance, using the verb *danced* instead of *moved* helps the reader picture the movement of the clouds in a different way.

- Explain that giving human traits, such as dancing, to nonhuman objects in writing is called *personification*.

- Write the sentence on the board:

  The wind howled at me as I rode my bicycle.

- Ask students which nonhuman object is being personified (wind). Then, ask them which word makes it an example of personification (howled). Discuss the meaning of the sentence. If students need additional practice, follow the same procedure with these examples:

  The walls whispered the family's secrets.

  The morning sun smiled on the parade.

  The trees waved in the wind.

Name _____ Date _____

Personification

Personification is giving human qualities to something that is not human.

Without personification: The old train slowly pulled into the station.

With personification: The old train <u>coughed</u> and <u>wheezed</u> as it pulled into the station.

Read each sentence. Write *yes* if the sentence includes personification. Write *no* if the sentence does not include personification.

1. _____ Blue skies smiled down on us.

2. _____ The sand under our feet was hot.

3. _____ The full moon observed the small town.

4. _____ The camera loves me; I always look great!

5. _____ The leaves fell on the ground.

6. _____ The tulips waved at us as we crossed the field.

7. _____ The rain danced on the pavement.

8. _____ The fallen snow yelled, "Come outside and build a snowman!"

9. _____ The cool water in the swimming pool invited us in.

10. _____ The airplane landed at the airport.

11. Select one sentence that is *not* an example of personification. Rewrite it so that it includes personification.

_____

_____

Step Up to Writing · CD-104384 · © Carson-Dellosa

Personification

Personification is giving human qualities to something that is not human.

Without personification: The old train slowly pulled into the station.

With personification: The old train <u>coughed</u> and <u>wheezed</u> as it pulled into the station.

Rewrite each sentence so that it includes personification. Replace the underlined word or words with words that describe a human action.

1. The rainbow <u>sparkled</u> in the bright sky. _____

_____

2. The flowers <u>moved</u> as I walked through the garden. _____

_____

3. The spotlight <u>shines</u> on the performers on the stage. _____

_____

4. The wooden bat <u>hit</u> the ball. _____

_____

5. The rocket <u>launched</u> into the dark sky. _____

_____

6. The old bench <u>made a noise</u> when I sat on it to relax. _____

_____

 Extra: On another sheet of paper, write examples of personification using these objects:

car   door   piano

Personification

Personification is giving human qualities to something that is nonhuman.

Without personification: The old train slowly pulled into the station.

With personification: The old train <u>coughed</u> and <u>wheezed</u> as it pulled into the station.

Read the word bank of nonhuman objects and human actions. Combine one object and one related action. Make five word pairs. Use each word pair to write an example of personification.

Example: The leaves whispered as the children quietly walked through them.

Nonhuman Objects		Human Actions	
boat	bus	cry	dance
chair	lamp	grab	juggle
leaves	ocean	laugh	moan
puddle	rain	sing	sleep
roses	snowflake	swallow	tickle
stars	storm	whisper	wink

1. _____

2. _____

3. _____

4. _____

5. _____

 Extra: Choose a previous writing assignment. Rewrite one sentence to include an example of personification.

Punctuation

Mini-Lesson

Authors must use correct punctuation to clearly communicate their thoughts to the reader. This lesson reviews the four types of sentences and corresponding punctuation marks, as well as two rules for comma usage.

Mini-Lesson:

- Review the four types of sentences and ending punctuation marks.

Types of Sentences	
1. A **declarative sentence** makes a statement. It ends with a period. *The clown juggled four balls.*	2. An **interrogative sentence** asks a question. It ends with a question mark. *Did you like the puppet show?*
3. An **exclamatory sentence** makes a statement with strong emotion. It ends with an exclamation point. *That show was awesome!*	4. An **imperative sentence** gives a direction or a command. It ends with a period or an exclamation point. *Please return to your seat.*

- Tell students that a comma helps the reader know which words go together in a sentence.

- Write the rules for commas on the board and explain them to students.

    1. Use a comma to separate the elements in a series (three or more things).
    I had salad, chicken, and a baked potato for dinner.

    2. Use commas after introductory clauses. These clauses provide background information for the main part of the sentence. Common starter words are: *after, although, as, if, because, before, since, then, though, until,* and *when.*
    After we eat dinner, I would like to go for a short walk.

- Write punctuation marks (periods, commas, exclamation points, and question marks) on self-stick notes and give them to students. Write sentences on the board and ask individual students to place punctuation where it belongs.

    Examples:

    Can we play outside

    You scored the winning goal

Punctuation

A **punctuation mark** indicates a stop or pause between groups of words. Punctuation marks help the reader make sense of written words.

There are four types of sentences.

A **declarative sentence** makes a statement. It ends with a period.

An **interrogative sentence** asks a question. It ends with a question mark.

An **exclamatory sentence** shows strong emotion. It ends with an exclamation point.

An **imperative sentence** gives a command. It ends with a period or an exclamation point.

Write an example of each type of sentence. Use the correct punctuation mark.

1. Declarative: _____

2. Interrogative: _____

3. Exclamatory: _____

4. Imperative: _____

Commas let the reader know which words should be read together and when to pause.

Write *yes* if commas are where they should be in each sentence. Write *no* if any commas are missing.

5. _____ I saw Grant, Melissa and Jacob at the mall.

6. _____ Because we ran out of food, I went grocery shopping.

7. _____ I forgot to buy the bread, milk, and sugar.

8. _____ If you want to play soccer, you must do well in school.

9. _____ Since Sheila was running late she decided not to pick up breakfast.

10. _____ My guitar drums and flute are stored in the basement.

Punctuation

A **punctuation mark** indicates a stop or pause between groups of words. Commas let the reader know which words should be read together and when a pause is necessary. Use commas to separate elements in a series (three or more things) and after introductory clauses.

Examples: I would like to order a taco, chips, and water.

Although I am sleepy, I will stay up to watch the movie.

The commas in the sentences are missing. Rewrite each sentence and add commas.

1. My uncle visited Big Ben the Tower Bridge and Buckingham Palace. _____

_____

2. Until my sister learns to behave in restaurants we will be eating at home. _____

_____

_____

3. Before we leave let's make sure that we have everything we need. _____

_____

4. I ate eggs pineapple and toast for breakfast. _____

_____

5. The weather is cool now but it will warm up later today. _____

_____

6. During a fire drill we must listen carefully to the teacher. _____

_____

7. She is allergic to cheese yogurt and milk. _____

_____

8. Panthers zebras and lions live in the local zoo. _____

_____

Punctuation

A **punctuation mark** indicates a stop or pause between groups of words. Commas let the reader know which words should be read together or when a pause is necessary. Use commas to separate elements in a series (three or more things) and after introductory clauses.

Examples: I would like to order a taco, chips, and water.

Although I am sleepy, I will stay up to watch the movie.

The paragraph is missing punctuation. Add the correct punctuation marks.

Kelly Allison Brandon and I wanted to go to the movies After our parents agreed to take us we made plans to meet at the theater on Saturday Kelly arrived first Allison and Brandon arrived immediately after By the time I got there everyone was in line to buy snacks Brandon ordered nachos popcorn and a large lemonade I could not believe that he planned to eat so much The rest of us decided to share a large popcorn Then it was time to go inside the theater We sat in the first row The theater was empty so we spent the entire time whispering and giggling I could not even tell you what the movie was about After it ended we said good-bye and headed home If our parents agree we will get together again next week

Subjects and Predicates

Mini-Lesson

Authors form complete sentences by including at least one subject and one predicate in each sentence. In this lesson, students will practice identifying and forming sentences with complete subjects and complete predicates.

Mini-Lesson:

- Explain to students that sentences contain two parts—the subject and the predicate. The complete subject contains all of the words that tell whom or what the sentence is about. The complete predicate contains all of the words that tell what the subject is or does.

- Write the sentence on the board: The young colt galloped across the field.

- Tell students that *the young colt* is what the sentence is about, so it is the complete subject. *Galloped across the field* explains what the colt does, so it is the complete predicate.

- Write sentences on sentence strips, color-coding the sentences so that all subjects are written in one color and all predicates are written in another color. Then, divide the class into two groups. Give one group the subjects. Give the other group the predicates.

  Examples that can be written on sentence strips:

  1. | The sweet smell of honey | | filled the air. |

  2. | The children in my neighborhood | | played outside until sunset. |

  3. | Knee pads | | protect you from serious injuries. |

- Have each student find a match to complete her sentence. Once students have found their matches, have each pair read the new sentence to the class. Explain that without a subject and a predicate, a sentence is not complete.

Extension

Review the definitions of a simple subject and a simple predicate. A simple subject is the main noun in a complete subject, and a simple predicate is the main verb in the complete predicate. Have students identify the simple subjects and the simple predicates in the sentences they formed with partners.

Name _____ Date _____

Subjects and Predicates

Sentences contain two parts: the subject and the predicate. The **complete subject** contains all of the words that tell whom or what the sentence is about. The **complete predicate** contains all of the words that tell what the subject is or does.

Write *S* if the word group is the subject. Write *P* if the word group is the predicate.

1. _____ the book

2. _____ likes to read

3. _____ plays football

4. _____ my friend

5. _____ old cars

6. _____ chased her kite

Write a complete subject for each sentence.

7. _____ likes to eat carrots.

8. _____ enjoys the cool breeze.

9. _____ is a great friend.

Write a complete predicate for each sentence.

10. The young eagle _____ .

11. Forest rangers _____ .

12. My trip to the museum _____ .

Subjects and Predicates

Sentences contain two parts: the subject and the predicate. The **complete subject** contains all of the words that tell whom or what the sentence is about. The **complete predicate** contains all of the words that tell what the subject is or does.

Underline each complete subject. Draw a box around each complete predicate.

1. Polar bear fur is water-resistant.

2. Rough paws prevent polar bears from slipping on the ice.

3. Large bears paddle with their front paws.

4. Many polar bears grow to be 10 feet tall.

5. Sometimes a polar bear stalks its prey.

6. Seals are their main diet.

7. The polar bear population is getting smaller.

8. Polar bears sleep seven to eight hours at a time.

9. Polar bears nap just about anywhere.

10. Snow geese do not run away from polar bears.

Subjects and Predicates

Sentences contain two parts: the subject and the predicate. The **complete subject** contains all of the words that tell whom or what the sentence is about. The **complete predicate** contains all of the words that tell what the subject is or does.

Use these nouns and verbs to write sentences with complete subjects and complete predicates.

1. car   roar

    _____

2. birds   flock

    _____

3. helmets   ride

    _____

4. students   run

    _____

5. glasses   break

    _____

Draw a box around each complete subject. Circle each complete predicate.

6. The gentle manatee lives in shallow water.

7. Most West Indian manatees live in Florida.

8. They look for food at the water's surface.

9. The average adult manatee is three meters (9.8 feet) long.

10. Manatees eat all types of plants.

 Extra: Draw one line under each simple subject and two lines under each simple predicate in sentences 6.–10.

Adjectives and Adverbs

Mini-Lesson

Authors use adjectives and adverbs to describe story elements. The effective use of adjectives and adverbs can add vivid detail, description, and clarity to writing.

Mini-Lesson:

- Write the sentence on the board:

    Young Isabel quickly ran through the green forest.

- Ask students to identify the nouns in the sentence (Isabel, forest). Then, ask students which words describe the nouns (young, green). Explain to students that an adjective is a word that describes a noun. An adjectives tells what kind, which one, or how many.

- Ask students to identify the verb in the sentence (ran). Then, ask them to describe how Isabel ran (quickly). Explain that a word that describes a verb is called an adverb. An adverb tells how, when, or where.

- Write the sentences on the board.

    The excited coach ran inside. (excited = what kind)

    The best skiers raced swiftly down the slopes. (best = which ones)

    Three ducks constantly dipped their heads in the pond. (three = how many)

- Have students come to the board and circle the adjectives. Then, have them identify whether each adjective tells what kind, which one, or how many

- Ask students to identify the adverbs in the sentences and whether each adverb tells how, when, or where (swiftly = how, constantly = when, inside = where).

Extension

Write several sentences on the board. Leave blanks for adjectives and adverbs. Have students come to the board and fill in each blank with an appropriate word.

Examples:

The _____ student studied his spelling words.

The sailor _____ saluted her captain.

Adjectives and Adverbs

Adjectives are words that describe nouns. An adjective tells how many, what kind, or which one. **Adverbs** are words that describe verbs. An adverb tells how, when, or where.

Example: Tom carefully polished the heavy, glass mirror.
Heavy and *glass* are adjectives. *Carefully* is an adverb.

Circle the adjectives. Remember, an adjective tells how many, what kind, or which one.

ice   shiny

strong   many

quick   girl

seven   jump

tall   dark

Circle the adverbs. Remember, an adverb describes how, when, or where.

yesterday   hungrily

blue   now

swamp   sad

outside   speedily

slowly   fly

Write two sentences using two circled adjectives.

1. _____

2. _____

Write two sentences using two circled adverbs.

3. _____

4. _____

Adjectives and Adverbs

Adjectives are words that describe nouns. An adjective tells how many, what kind, or which one. **Adverbs** are words that describe verbs. An adverb tells how, when, or where.

Example: Tom carefully polished the heavy, glass mirror.
Heavy and _glass_ are adjectives. _Carefully_ is an adverb.

Draw an arrow from each adjective to the underlined noun that it describes.

1. The calm <u>water</u> is inviting.

2. The large <u>bird</u> is searching for a tasty <u>worm</u>.

3. I love the smell of fresh <u>coffee</u> in the morning.

4. Last night, I counted three bright <u>stars</u> in the sky.

5. Have you seen my green and purple <u>socks</u>?

Draw an arrow from each adverb to the underlined verb that it describes.

6. The boys <u>behaved</u> well at the party.

7. My family and I <u>will visit</u> the zoo tomorrow.

8. The children <u>stood</u> nearby.

9. Mr. Krenz politely <u>explained</u> the class rules.

10. The school bus <u>arrived</u> late.

Name _____ Date _____

Adjectives and Adverbs

Adjectives are words that describe nouns. An adjective tells how many, what kind, or which one. **Adverbs** are words that describe verbs. An adverb tells how, when, or where.

Example: Tom carefully polished the heavy, glass mirror.
            Heavy and *glass* are adjectives. *Carefully* is an adverb.

Add two adjectives to each sentence. Rewrite the sentences.

1. The swan ate a fish. _____

_____

2. The child did not want to leave the party. _____

_____

3. The airplane is in the sky. _____

_____

4. Monkeys climbed the tree. _____

_____

Add an adverb to each sentence. Rewrite the sentences.

5. The train arrived. _____

_____

6. The dancers practiced their routine. _____

_____

7. Jason walked into the shop. _____

_____

8. The boy went to the main office. _____

_____

 Extra: Choose a previous writing assignment. Rewrite two sentences using an adjective and an adverb in each sentence.

● ● ●

Dialogue: Using Correct Punctuation

Mini-Lesson

Authors often use dialogue to create interest and authenticity in their writing. This lesson explains the use of correct punctuation marks when writing dialogue.

Mini-Lesson:

- Ask students how they can tell when characters in a story are speaking.

- Explain that quotation marks are used around the exact words that someone says. For example, "That's a lovely dress you have on," remarked Mrs. Cox. The quotation marks do not include *remarked Mrs. Cox* because those words are not spoken by Mrs. Cox. *Remarked* is the dialogue tag that tells the reader who is speaking.

- Have students look through books and novels that include dialogue. Tell them to pay close attention to the punctuation used when the characters speak.

- Write these rules on the board:

> 1. Use quotation marks around a speaker's exact words.
>
> 2. Capitalize the first word that a speaker says.
>
> 3. Use one set of quotation marks for dialogue that is not interrupted with narrative. For example, "I really liked the scenery. The props were fantastic," replied Elena.
>
> 4. When a dialogue tag is placed between the parts of the quotation, put quotation marks around each part. For example, "Yes," said Joan, "that was a great show."
>
> 5. If dialogue is broken up by a dialogue tag and the second part of the quotation is a separate sentence, begin the second part with a capital letter. For example, "I liked it too," said Kim. "Maybe I will see it again next week."

- Review these rules with students. On the board, write sentences that need quotation marks. Ask students to come to the board and add punctuation where needed.

> **Note**: If students are struggling with dialogue punctuation, introduce the rules in segments. Begin with quotation marks and capitalization. Follow with dialogue tags and commas.

Dialogue: Using Correct Punctuation

Quotation marks are used around the exact words that someone speaks.

Examples: "How was your day today?" asked Mom.

"It was great," replied Tiffany. "I had a lot of fun."

Rewrite the sentences. Add quotation marks and capital letters where needed.

1. are you ready to leave? asked Grandpa. _____

_____

2. I had a huge breakfast this morning, said Miguel. _____

_____

3. Libby said, wait for me! I don't want to be late. _____

_____

4. I stubbed my toe on my way to the bus stop, moaned Jack. _____

_____

5. hooray! I won the race! exclaimed Riley. _____

_____

6. Would you like a slice of apple pie? asked Mrs. Havel. _____

_____

7. Ryan said, I would like to go for a swim. _____

_____

8. Parker replied, no, I have not seen your lunch box. _____

_____

Dialogue: Using Correct Punctuation

Quotation marks are used around the exact words that someone speaks.

Examples: "How was your day today?" asked Mom.

"It was great," replied Tiffany. "I had a lot of fun."

Rewrite the sentences. Add quotation marks and capital letters where needed.

1. i thought about taking a bus. But, I finally decided to take an airplane, said Emily.

_____

_____

2. I am not sure, sighed Tony. I just can't remember where I left my keys. _____

_____

_____

3. the treasure is hidden in the forest, whispered the prince. _____

_____

4. Did you see where Melinda went? asked Tyler. I want to invite her over for lunch.

_____

_____

5. Sue asked, do you know how to grow an herb garden? _____

_____

6. I want to learn to play the cello, said Maria. Will you teach me? _____

_____

7. jelly beans are my favorite! shouted Daniel. I love the cherry-flavored ones.

_____

_____

Dialogue: Using Correct Punctuation

Quotation marks are used around the exact words that someone speaks. Begin a new paragraph with each change of speaker in dialogue.

Example: Anthony saw Jennifer getting into a car across the street. "Hey, Jennifer," said Anthony. "How's it going?"

"Pretty good, thanks," replied Jennifer. "How are you?"

"Great!" said Anthony.

Rewrite the passage using dialogue to show when a character speaks. Use correct punctuation and begin a new paragraph when the speaker changes.

When Megan and I went to the zoo, Megan asked me if I wanted to see the gorillas. I thought that would be fun, so we walked to the monkey habitat. Two large gorillas were resting peacefully on the grass. I told Megan that I could not believe how large gorillas could get. Megan said that she expected them to be larger! I was getting hungry, so I asked Megan if we could eat lunch. She suggested burgers. I mentioned that I'd like to see the tigers, so we made plans to see them after lunch.

_____

_____

_____

_____

_____

_____

_____

_____

_____

Sentence Variety

Good authors use conjunctions to make their writing flow and to connect ideas that belong together. Conjunctions combine simple sentences and vary sentence structure.

Mini-Lesson:

- Write the sentences on the board. Ask students to read them aloud.

  The girl went to the store.

  The girl bought lemonade.

  The girl drank it quickly.

  The girl was still thirsty.

- Ask students to share what they notice about these sentences. Explain that repeating the beginning of the simple sentences does not interest the reader. Combining sentences with conjunctions will make sentences more appealing.

Conjunctions Word Bank			
after	although	and	as
because	before	but	or
so	when	while	yet

- Write the conjunctions from the word bank on the board and ask students which they might use to combine the sentences.

Examples:

The girl went to the store and bought lemonade. She drank it quickly, but she was still thirsty.

The girl went to the store, bought lemonade, and drank it quickly. But, she was still thirsty.

- Write several sentences on the board. Have students use conjunctions to rewrite them.

Examples:

The bear jumped into the river. The bear went for a swim.

Grace finished her homework. Grace went outside.

Jonathan counted his coins. Jonathan paid for the notebook.

Sentence Variety

Combining simple sentences with a **conjunction** can make an author's writing flow.

Example: The boy picked up his new pencil. The boy used it to write a poem.

Better: The boy picked up his new pencil <u>and</u> used it to write a poem.

Circle the conjunction in each sentence.

1. The tiger was hungry, so he went hunting.

2. Fish have fins and breathe through gills.

3. She hummed while her sister sang.

4. The cat curled into a ball although she was not sleepy.

5. He put on his helmet before he put on his in-line skates.

6. The bird flew away because the noise startled him.

7. The duck quacked as she swam in the lake.

8. The bride smiled when the photographer took her picture.

9. Penguins are birds, but they do not fly.

10. You may draw a picture or write a story.

Extra: Use a conjunction to combine each pair of simple sentences. Write the new sentences.

The horse ran into the barn. The horse neighed loudly. _____

_____

She went to the grocery store. She bought some apples. _____

_____

Sentence Variety

Combining simple sentences with a **conjunction** can make an author's writing flow.

Example: The boy picked up his new pencil. The boy used it to write a poem.

Better: The boy picked up his new pencil <u>and</u> used it to write a poem.

Use a conjunction from the word bank to combine each pair of simple sentences. Write the new sentences. You may use a conjunction more than once.

Conjunctions Word Bank					
after	although	and	as	because	before
but	or	so	when	while	yet

1. Sarah wanted to go swimming. It rained. _____

_____

2. The car broke down. I took a taxi. _____

_____

3. The man was tired. The man sat on a bench. _____

_____

4. It started raining. I opened my umbrella. _____

_____

5. I watered the plant. It wilted. _____

_____

6. The baby cried. The baby was hungry. _____

_____

7. Jeremy bought some milk. He still had some left. _____

_____

8. The boy started a new painting. His first painting was drying. _____

_____

Sentence Variety

Combining simple sentences with a **conjunction** can make an author's writing flow.

Example: The boy had a new pencil. He picked it up. The boy used it to write a poem.

Better: The boy picked up his new pencil <u>and</u> used it to write a poem.

Use conjunctions from the word bank to combine the simple sentences. Remove unnecessary words or change the word order. Write the new sentences. You may use a conjunction more than once.

Conjunctions Word Bank					
after	although	and	as	because	before
but	or	so	when	while	yet

1. Chang took a deep breath. Chang smelled something good. Chang realized that it was chocolate chip cookies. _____

_____

2. The alarm rang. Talia got out of bed. She went to the kitchen. _____

_____

_____

3. I was hungry. I ate a banana. I felt better. _____

_____

4. I finished my homework. I wanted to play outside. My mom told me to put away my books first. _____

_____

5. The chimpanzee squealed. The chimpanzee bounced up and down. The chimpanzee was hungry. _____

_____

_____

Children's Literature

Because of Winn-Dixie by Kate DiCamillo. Candlewick: Somerville, MA, 2009.

Brave Irene by William Steig. Farrar, Straus and Giroux: New York, NY, 1988.

Charlotte's Web by E. B. White. HarperCollins: New York, NY, 2001.

Cloudy With a Chance of Meatballs by Judi Barrett. Aladdin: New York, NY, 1982.

Come On, Rain by Karen Hesse. Scholastic: New York, NY, 1999.

Dear Mr. Blueberry by Simon James. Aladdin: New York, NY, 1996.

Dear Mr. Henshaw by Beverly Cleary. HarperCollins: New York, NY, 2000.

Diary of a Wimpy Kid by Jeff Kinney. Abrams Books for Young Readers: New York, NY, 2007.

Earrings! by Judith Viorst. Aladdin: New York, NY, 1993.

Freckle Juice by Judy Blume. Random House Children's Books: New York, NY, 1978.

Grandfather's Journey by Allan Say. Houghton Mifflin Harcourt: New York, NY, 2008.

The Great Kapok Tree by Lynne Cherry. Houghton Mifflin Harcourt: New York, NY, 2000.

James and the Giant Peach by Roald Dahl. Puffin: New York, NY, 2007.

Julius, Baby of the World by Kevin Henkes. HarperCollins: New York, NY, 1995.

Jumanji by Chris Van Allsburg. Houghton Mifflin Harcourt: New York, NY, 1981.

Lilly's Purple Plastic Purse by Kevin Henkes. HarperCollins: New York, NY, 1996.

Mailing May by Michael O. Tunnell. HarperCollins: New York, NY, 2000.

Matilda by Roald Dahl. Puffin: New York, NY, 2007.

Miss Nelson Is Missing! by James Marshall. Houghton Mifflin Harcourt: New York, NY, 1985.

Night in the Country by Cynthia Rylant. Aladdin: New York, NY, 1991.

Old Penn Station by William Low. Henry Holt and Company: New York, NY, 2007.

Owl Moon by Jane Yolen. Philomel: New York, NY, 1987.

The Pain and the Great One by Judy Blume. Random House Children's Books: New York, NY, 1985.

The Paper Bag Princess by Robert Munsch. Annick Press: Toronto, ON, 1992.

Pink and Say by Patricia Polacco. Philomel: New York, NY, 1994.

The Polar Express by Chris Van Allsburg. Houghton Mifflin Harcourt: New York, NY, 1985.

Ramona the Pest by Beverly Cleary. HarperCollins: New York, NY, 1992.

Red Riding Hood by James Marshall. Puffin: New York, NY, 1993.

The Relatives Came by Cynthia Rylant. Aladdin: New York, NY, 1993.

Sarah, Plain and Tall by Patricia MacLachlan. Gale Group: New York, NY, 2005.

Tales of a Fourth Grade Nothing by Judy Blume. Puffin: New York, NY, 2007.

Tar Beach by Faith Ringgold. Crown Publishing: New York, NY, 1991.

A Taste of Blackberries by Doris Buchanan Smith. HarperCollins: New York, NY, 1992.

There's a Boy in the Girls' Bathroom by Louis Sachar. Dell Yearling: New York, NY, 1988.

Thunder Cake by Patricia Polacco. Putnam Juvenile: New York, NY, 1997.

The True Story of the 3 Little Pigs by Jon Scieszka. Puffin: New York, NY, 1996.

Where the Wild Things Are by Maurice Sendak. HarperCollins: New York, NY, 1988.

Answer Key

Page 9
Answers will vary.

Extra: Answers will vary.

Page 10
1. Answers will vary but may include:

    Hibernation is a major part of a black bear's life. Black bears remain in a sleeplike condition throughout the winter months. They find dens or caves to hibernate in. When it is hibernating, a bear's body temperature drops about 10 degrees. Hibernating is important because it helps bears survive a season when food is limited.

2. Answers will vary but may include:

    Black bears are omnivores. They eat both plants and animals. Many bears catch fish, such as salmon, from rivers and streams. They eat nuts and berries. Insects, from ants to termites, are also an important part of their diet. Eating both plants and animals helps bears get the nutrition they need.

Page 11
Answers will vary.

Extra: Answers will vary.

Page 14
Answers will vary.

Extra: Answers will vary.

Pages 15-16
Answers will vary.

Pages 19-21
Answers will vary.

Page 23
1. A. yes   B. no
2. A. yes   B. no
3. A. no   B. yes
4. A. no   B. yes

Page 24-25
Answers will vary.

Page 27
1. A. yes   B. no
2. A. no   B. yes
3. A. yes   B. no
4. A. yes   B. no

Pages 28-29
Answers will vary.

Page 31
1. A. yes   B. no
2. A. no   B. yes
3. A. no   B. yes
4. A. yes   B. no

Pages 32-33
Answers will vary.

Page 35
1. A. yes   B. no
2. A. no   B. yes
3. A. yes   B. no
4. A. yes   B. no

Pages 36-37
Answers will vary.

Page 39

Did you know that you can plant a sunflower seed inside a cup? It is simple and fun! <u>First</u>, gather the following materials: a clear, plastic cup; a wet paper towel; and a sunflower seed. <u>Next</u>, place the paper towel inside the cup. <u>At this point</u>, make sure that the paper towel covers the entire inside of the cup. Place the seed on the paper towel and fold the paper towel over the seed. <u>Then</u>, place the cup near a window with a lot of sunlight shining through. If your plant does not get enough sunlight, it will not be able to grow. It will take three weeks for your seed to sprout. <u>Meanwhile</u>, you can record any changes that you observe. <u>Finally</u>, you will be able to see your sunflower flourish!

1. First
2. Next
3. At this point
4. Then
5. Meanwhile
6. Finally

Page 39, continued

Extra: Answers will vary but should note that planting the seed would be more difficult without the time-order words.

Page 40

Answers will vary but may include:

Monday mornings are always hectic for me. Mom and Dad have a lot for me to do before I can leave for school. <u>First</u>, I have to take a warm shower. This always helps me wake up and get ready for the day ahead. <u>Next</u>, I put on my clothes. This part is easy because I wear my school uniform each day. <u>Then</u>, I have to make my bed. I can't even think about having breakfast until I make my bed. <u>Now</u>, I have to wake my little brother. He gets to sleep later than I do. I try to wake him slowly. <u>First</u>, I whisper his name. <u>Next</u>, I give him a gentle push. If that doesn't work, I have no choice but to yell, "Tommy, get up!" That usually does the trick. <u>Eventually</u> my stomach starts growling, so I eat a bowl of cereal. On Monday mornings, we have no time for fluffy pancakes. I <u>then</u> brush my teeth and comb my hair. I can <u>finally</u> head off to school!

Page 41

Answers will vary.

Page 44

Answers will vary.

Extra: Answers will vary.

Pages 45–46

Answers will vary.

Pages 48–49

Answers will vary.

Page 50

Answers will vary.

Extra: Answers will vary.

Page 52

Answers will vary.

Extra: Answers will vary.

Page 53

Answers will vary.

Extra: Answers will vary.

Page 54

Answers will vary.

Extra: Answers will vary.

Pages 56–58

Answers will vary.

Page 61

Answers written on lines will vary, but labels should be in order: heading, greeting, body, closing, and signature.

Pages 62–63

Answers will vary.

Page 65

123 Dade Pine Ct.
Miami, FL 33016
February 7, 2011

Mrs. Hurns
Palm Elementary School
456 Bobcat Way
Miami, FL 32986

Dear Mrs. Hurns:

I would like to ask you to add a new food to the menu. I would especially like to have veggie pizzas as part of our school lunch.

The students in my fourth-grade class like the chicken, hamburgers, and spaghetti and meatballs that we eat for lunch, but we would like a meatless choice too. Veggie pizza can be made quickly and would not take up too much time. The cafeteria staff might be happy to make something new that everyone can enjoy. The ingredients in this meal are also part of a well-balanced diet. This will help us grow strong and healthy.

Thank you for taking the time to read my suggestion. I hope that you will think about it.

Sincerely,

Eva Davis
Eva Davis

Extra: Labels should be in order: heading, inside address, greeting, body, closing, and signature.

Page 66

Answers will vary.

Page 67

Answers will vary.

Extra: Labels should be in order: heading, inside address, greeting, body, closing, and signature.

Pages 69–70

Answers will vary.

Page 71

Answers will vary.

Extra: Answers will vary.

Page 73

1. no
2. yes
3. no

Page 74

Answers will vary but may include:

Test Day

It was the big day. Test Day! I was nervous as I walked into my class. I walked to my desk and sat down. ~~Ben walked in, wearing a blue and white shirt. He has brown hair and freckles.~~ I opened my backpack and took out my pencils. I wanted to be ready when Ms. Kincaid started the test. I had butterflies in my stomach. I tried to remember what my mother had told me at breakfast, "Relax and do your best. That is the most important thing." ~~I had cereal for breakfast. My brother was there too, but he doesn't like cereal.~~ The rest of my classmates finally arrived. Ms. Kincaid said hello to everyone and gave us a pep talk. ~~She is a great teacher. She has worked hard to get us ready for Test Day. She is always in a good mood. My teacher last year wasn't like that. I want to be a teacher when I grow up, but I want to be like Ms. Kincaid.~~ As Ms. Kincaid passed out the tests, I took out my lucky penny and put it in my pocket. ~~My dad gave it to me when I was four. I put it in the pocket of my dress the night of my recital, right before I went on stage. I wore a beautiful pink~~

Page 74, continued

~~dress with matching shoes that night.~~ It was time! We began our test. I was super relieved that I knew most of the answers! My studying had paid off! A little later, Ms. Kincaid called time and asked Mary to help her collect the tests. ~~Mary is new at our school.~~ As I turned in my test, I breathed a sigh of relief. It was over! I had done it! ~~I put my penny away and got ready for recess. Today we were going to play kickball, and I was excited because kickball is my favorite sport.~~

Page 75

Answers will vary.

Page 77

1. B.
2. B.
3. B.
4. A.
5. B.
6. A.
7. B.
8. A.

Pages 78–79

Answers will vary.

Page 81

Answers will vary.

Page 82

1. The teacher is strict.
   Clues: stated firmly, serious look

2. John is excited.
   Clues: jumped out of bed, continued to smile, can't wait to hang out

3. Anna is intelligent.
   Clues: always earns an A, spelling bee champion, great student

Extra: Answers will vary.

Page 83

Answers will vary.

Extra: Answers will vary.

Pages 85–87

Answers will vary.

Answer Key, continued

Page 89
1. A. T   B. S
2. A. S   B. T
3. A. T   B. S
4. A. T   B. S
5. A. S   B. T
6. A. S   B. T

Page 90–91
Answers will vary.

Page 93
Answers will vary but may include:
1. begged
2. admitted, confessed
3. giggled
4. warned, explained
5. whispered
6. explained
7. cheered
8. explained
9. warned, explained
10. explained

Page 94
1. C.
2. A.
3. B.
4.–10. Answers will vary.

Page 95
Answers will vary.

Page 97
1. government office
2. family member
3. friend
4. teacher

Extra: Answers will vary.

Page 98
Answers will vary.

Extra: Answers will vary.

Page 99
Answers will vary.

Page 102
1. A. yes   B. no
2. A. no   B. yes
3. A. yes   B. no

Page 103
Answers will vary but may include:

Sometimes, I wish my little brother would stop following me around. <u>I know that sounds mean, but it's true!</u> If you had a little brother like Erik, you would feel the same way. <u>Trust me.</u> This morning, I was dressed and ready for school. Just as I was about to grab my things and catch the bus, <u>who drops an entire bowl of wet, soggy, mushy, disgusting cereal on my backpack? Erik, of course. He is like a two-year-old tornado!</u>

Extra: Answers will vary.

Page 104
Answers will vary.

Extra: Answers will vary.

Pages 106–108
Answers will vary.

Pages 110–112
Answers will vary.

Page 114
1. flew
2. scolded
3. terrified
4. wheezed
5. skipped
6. danced
7. rode
8. performed
9. chased
10. relaxed

Page 115
1. gasped
2. floated
3. poured
4. scribbled
5. explored
6. grumbled
7. flopped
8. peeked

Page 116
Answers will vary.

Answer Key, continued

Pages 118
1. M
2. S
3. S
4. M
5. S
6. M
7. S
8. S
9.–10. Answers will vary.

Pages 119–120
Answers will vary.

Page 122
1. roar
2. smack
3. Whirr
4. toot
5. meow
6. buzz
7. Drip
8. honk
9. Ding-dong
10. slurp
11.–12. Answers will vary.

Page 123
Answers will vary.

Page 124
Answers will vary.

Extra: Answers will vary.

Page 126
Answers will vary.

Page 127
1. B.
2. A.
3. A.
4. B.
5. A.
6. B.

Page 128
Answers will vary but may include:
1. easy to do
2. speechless; can't find the right words
3. old; far along in life
4. go to bed
5. ready to listen
6.–8. Answers will vary.

Extra: Answers will vary.

Page 130
1. yes
2. no
3. yes
4. yes
5. no
6. yes
7. yes
8. yes
9. yes
10. no
11. Answers will vary.

Page 131
Answers will vary.

Extra: Answers will vary.

Page 132
Answers will vary.

Extra: Answers will vary.

Page 134
1.–4. Answers will vary.
5. no
6. yes
7. yes
8. yes
9. no
10. no

Page 135
1. My uncle visited Big Ben, the Tower Bridge, and Buckingham Palace.

2. Until my sister learns to behave in restaurants, we will be eating at home.

3. Before we leave, let's make sure that we have everything we need.

4. I ate eggs, pineapple, and toast for breakfast.

5. The weather is cool now, but it will warm up later today.

6. During a fire drill, we must listen carefully to the teacher.

7. She is allergic to cheese, yogurt, and milk

8. Panthers, zebras, and lions live in the local zoo.

Answer Key, continued

Page 136

Kelly, Allison, Brandon, and I wanted to go to the movies. After our parents agreed to take us, we made plans to meet at the theater on Saturday. Kelly arrived first. Allison and Brandon arrived immediately after. By the time I got there, everyone was in line to buy snacks. Brandon ordered nachos, popcorn, and a large lemonade. I could not believe that he planned to eat so much! The rest of us decided to share a large popcorn. Then, it was time to go inside the theater. We sat in the first row. The theater was empty, so we spent the entire time whispering and giggling. I could not even tell you what the movie was about! After it ended, we said good-bye and headed home. If our parents agree, we will get together next week.

Page 138

1. S
2. P
3. P
4. S
5. S
6. P
7.–12. Answers will vary.

Page 139

1. Polar bear fur | is water resistant. |
2. Rough paws | prevent polar bears from slipping on the ice. |
3. Large bears | paddle with their front paws. |
4. Many polar bears | grow to be 10 feet tall. |
5. Sometimes a polar bear | stalks its prey. |
6. Seals | are their main diet. |
7. The polar bear population | is getting smaller. |
8. Polar bears | sleep seven to eight hours at a time. |
9. Polar bears | nap just about anywhere. |
10. Snow geese | do not run away from polar bears. |

Page 140

1.–5. Answers will vary.

6. The gentle manatee | lives in shallow water. |
   Extra: manatee, lives
7. Most West Indian manatees | live in Florida. |
   Extra: manatees, live
8. They | look for food at the water's surface. |
   Extra: They, look
9. The average adult manatee | is three meters long. |
   Extra: manatee, is
10. Manatees | eat all types of plants. |
   Extra: Manatees, eat

Page 142

Adjectives: strong, quick, seven, tall, shiny, many, dark

Adverbs: yesterday, outside, slowly, hungrily, now, speedily

1.–4. Answers will vary.

Page 143

1. The calm water is inviting.
2. The large bird is searching for a tasty worm.
3. I love the smell of fresh coffee in the morning.
4. Last night, I counted three bright stars in the sky.
5. Have you seen my green and purple socks?
6. The boys behaved well at the party.
7. My family and I will visit the zoo tomorrow.
8. The children stood nearby.
9. Mr. Krenz politely explained the class rules.
10. The school bus arrived late.

Answer Key, continued

Page 144

Answers will vary.

Extra: Answers will vary.

Page 146

1. "Are you ready to leave?" asked Grandpa.
2. "I had a huge breakfast this morning," said Miguel.
3. Libby said, "Wait for me! I don't want to be late."
4. "I stubbed my toe on my way to the bus stop," moaned Jack.
5. "Hooray! I won the race!" exclaimed Riley.
6. "Would you like a slice of apple pie?" asked Mrs. Havel.
7. Ryan said, "I would like to go for a swim."
8. Parker replied, "No, I have not seen your lunch box."

Page 147

1. "I thought about taking a bus. But, I finally decided to take an airplane," said Emily.
2. "I am not sure," sighed Tony. "I just can't remember where I left my keys."
3. "The treasure is hidden in the forest," whispered the prince.
4. "Did you see where Melinda went?" asked Tyler. "I want to invite her over for lunch."
5. Sue asked, "Do you know how to grow an herb garden?"
6. "I want to learn to play the cello," said Maria. "Will you teach me?"
7. "Jelly beans are my favorite!" shouted Daniel. "I love the cherry-flavored ones."

Page 148

Answers will vary but may include:

When Megan and I went to the zoo, Megan asked, "Do you want to see the gorillas?" I thought that would be fun, so we walked to the monkey habitat. Two large gorillas were resting peacefully on the grass.

I told Megan, "I can't believe how large gorillas can get."

Megan said, "I expected them to be larger!"

I was getting hungry, so I asked, "Can we eat lunch?" Megan suggested burgers.

I said, "I'd like to see the tigers," so we made plans to see them after lunch.

Page 150

1. so
2. and
3. while
4. although
5. before
6. because
7. as
8. when
9. but
10. or

Extra: Answers will vary.

Page 151

Answers will vary, but may include:

1. Sarah wanted to go swimming, but it rained.
2. The car broke down, so I took a taxi.
3. The man was tired, so he sat on a bench.
4. It started raining, so I opened my umbrella.
5. I watered the plant because it wilted.
6. The baby cried because he was hungry.
7. Jeremy bought some milk, but he still had some left.
8. The boy started a new painting while his first painting was drying.

Page 152

Answers will vary but may include:

1. When Chang took a deep breath, he smelled something good and realized that it was chocolate chip cookies.
2. After the alarm rang, Talia got out of bed and went to the kitchen.
3. I was hungry, so I ate a banana, and I felt better.
4. I wanted to play outside after I finished my homework, but my mom told me to put away my books first.
5. The chimpanzee squealed and bounced up and down because she was hungry.